Debbie has taught me not to do hospitality but to *be* hospitable in every facet of my life. . . . This book is a gift for any ministry that is seeking to impart the heart of the Father through valuing, serving, and loving all individuals, communities, and nations.

DONNA BELL
YWAM Wollongong, Australia

A Cup of Cold Water is an incredible resource for home educators to use in a home economics course. We used this book as the foundation for an entire course, and it has made a lasting impression on our daughter's perception and practice of the art of hospitality.

DONNA MILES
Home educator and school teacher, Dallas, Texas

Since you weren't here to sign up for lunch, we will eat without you. That's the treatment I got at one mission center. . . . This book is great for helping you genuinely welcome and care for those who come from afar. I wish every host or hostess could read and apply the advice given in this book. Battle-weary missionaries will thank you for your efforts.

ROGER REECK
Wycliffe Bible Translators, La Ceiba, Honduras

Debbie has shown great skill in demonstrating God's ways and his delight in giving good gifts. . . . Whether through our daily lives in blessing those who come into our homes or through the doors of ministries where hospitality is our primary responsibility, there are great depths of joy to be found in giving "a cup of cold water."

LYNN GREEN
Youth With A Mission

Showing hospitality is not something we do; it is who we are and what we live. Debbie has done an amazing job helping new generation YWAMers understand the heart of God in living a lifestyle of hospitality. Her book is like a cup of cold water, refreshing every time!

MARJOLEIN COGHI
YWAM base leader, San José, Costa Rica

In 1 Timothy 3 and Titus 1, Paul includes hospitality as a requirement for spiritual leadership. Why is it so important? Because it expresses the heart of God to honor people and embrace what is new, foreign, or different. . . . I commend Debbie [Rottier] to you. Learn from her all you can about this important spiritual leadership gift—hospitality.

LOREN CUNNINGHAM
Founder, Youth With A Mission

A Cup of Cold Water is a must-read book. . . . Debbie Rottier gives a new perspective to hospitality, and I appreciate the understanding she gives to serving people from different nations.

SAMUEL LUFIYELE

African pastor serving an International Church, Edmonton, Canada

Hospitality is an essential ministry of unselfish giving that must be a mark of every believer. How did this ministry become a nonessential in so much of the Church? Debbie shines light on the subject with biblical exhortation, lots of great stories, and explanation of the "how-to." What a helpful book!

MARTI GREEN

Youth With A Mission

A *cup* OF

Cold Water

HOSPITALITY AT ITS BEST

DEBBIE ROTTIER

To Denise
Debbie Rottier
Mark 9:41

YWAM PUBLISHING
Seattle, Washington

YWAM Publishing is the publishing ministry of Youth With A Mission (YWAM), an international missionary organization of Christians from many denominations dedicated to presenting Jesus Christ to this generation. To this end, YWAM has focused its efforts in three main areas: (1) training and equipping believers for their part in fulfilling the Great Commission (Matthew 28:19), (2) personal evangelism, and (3) mercy ministry (medical and relief work).

For a free catalog of books and materials, call (425) 771–1153 or (800) 922–2143.
Visit us online at www.ywampublishing.com.

A Cup of Cold Water: Hospitality at Its Best
Copyright © 2002, 2012 by Debbie Rottier
Illustrations by Julie Bosacker
Second edition

Published by YWAM Publishing
a ministry of Youth With A Mission
PO Box 55787, Seattle, WA 98155–0787

Library of Congress Cataloging-in-Publication Data
Rottier, Debbie E.
    A cup of cold water : hospitality at its best.—2nd ed.
        p. cm.
    ISBN 978-1-57658-715-7
    1. Hospitality—Religious aspects—Christianity. 2. Youth with a Mission, Inc.—Anecdotes. I. Title.
    BV4647.H67R68 2012
    241'.671—dc23   2011051144

"Our YWAM Story: Love Feast Beginnings" on pages 125–127 used by permission. Copyright © 1998, 2001 by Tom Bloomer, with thanks to Al Akimoff and Reona Joly.

Please see page 173 for the copyright notices of all Bible versions used in this book.

First printing 2012

Printed in the United States of America

*To hospitality ministries around the world—from Africa
to Asia, and from Greenland to New Zealand*

contents

foreword

I have known Debbie Rottier for over thirty years. For much of that time, she has worked closely with me, leading out in the area of hospitality—hosting kings and dignitaries, children, and the masses—and doing it all with excellence.

Deb has traveled widely, practicing hospitality and teaching on the subject in a variety of contexts and cultures in Africa, Europe, Asia, North America, and the Pacific. She has a love for the nations, a love for people, and a heart to serve that is imparted through *A Cup of Cold Water.*

This book provides a very practical basis for hospitality, not from a Western viewpoint, but from a biblical intercultural perspective. It is my joy to highly recommend both the author and the material. As you read this book, I believe you will gain new insights into the heart of God, the way he values people, and the high calling of hospitality!

DARLENE CUNNINGHAM
Cofounder, Youth With A Mission

introduction

Thank you, friends, for reading this book. I have been with Youth With A Mission (YWAM) since 1982. Many of my life stories in this book will refer to my years in ministry with YWAM. However, all of us who are engaged in serving others will be able to glean from what is written.

As I wrote this book for my fellow YWAM hosts and hostesses, my heart was overwhelmed. I have been awed by the faithfulness of God's leading in my life through the ministry of hospitality. For me, it all began in the winter of 1982, when I was challenged to pray about working in hospitality. I didn't realize the power of hospitality as a ministry. But as I worked with my team leader, Eva Spengler, I soon saw the significance and influence of this ministry. My heart quickly filled with joy and excitement. "Yes, God!" I said. "This is what I want to do. I want to serve the saints, reach out to the lonely, and minister to those who bless our mission with their teachings." All of a sudden, the drudgery I had once felt of "just another day in hospitality" was replaced with anticipation for each new day, fresh with inspiration, creativity, and a continuous flow of the gifting God had instilled in me.

During my years in YWAM, I have had the privilege of working cross-culturally in many nations of the world. From Uganda to Indonesia, from the Netherlands to Hawaii—no matter where I've been, hospitality has been culturally relevant. Now, nearly three decades after my introduction to YWAM hospitality, I am still serving, still loving it, and still receiving new inspiration.

In presenting this book, it is my hope that the ministry of hospitality will become nearer and dearer to your heart and that you will discover new ways to serve those who come your way.

Two people who have come my way are YWAM founders Loren and Darlene Cunningham. I have worked with Loren and Darlene for almost thirty years, and they are very dear to me. Loren and Darlene have lived the example of hospitality, giving me an incredible model. They always have room for one more person in their home, their hearts, and their lives. They offer hospitality even when their schedule is already full, and they are the reason why it is important to me to champion this ministry and to share it. I believe that their example of service is why God has blessed YWAM, which is now the largest missionary organization in the world. From the Cunninghams, I have learned that there is always room for one more person—physically, spiritually, and mentally.

Hospitality has been a central focus of the YWAM ministry since its early days. In 1969 Loren and Darlene went to Lausanne, Switzerland, to establish the first Youth With A Mission Training School. Their first staff was a group of "pioneers." This little group began to put down roots, but long before they felt settled, God brought scores of people into the new community. Young, old, rich, poor—hundreds of people of all nationalities and ethnic origins were drawn to Lausanne.

Through the Word of God and the openness of her own heart, Darlene began to see that God wanted to honor these visitors and show his love through her. She was inspired by the ministry of the Evangelical Sisterhood of Mary in Darmstadt, Germany, who filled all they did with beauty and made an art form out of anticipating the needs of their guests. Challenged by the Lord to do a Bible study on hospitality, Darlene became convinced that this was not just good social protocol, but a ministry dear to God's heart.

Darlene began doing special things for visitors. For each guest she made a little card with a warm, loving greeting. She placed a basket of fruit on each nightstand just to say, "You're special to me and to the Lord." She prayed for each guest as she lovingly made up beds. These are still our values in YWAM today as we prepare for each guest.

Darlene made sure that guests were treated as King Jesus would be treated if he himself had visited Lausanne. Her simple expressions of hospitality reflected the love of Jesus Christ in a way that greatly blessed and ministered to people. Because of her loving actions, many were won to the Lord, and many were so deeply touched that they became missionaries or missions supporters.

In 1996 the base closed for renovation. Loren and Darlene arrived with a staff to rebuild it. My family and I were part of that team.

There was a lot of work to do. The building structure needed to be refurbished—it was drafty, noisy, and dusty. For my part, I set to work on a different foundation, that of reestablishing the hospitality ministry. I aspired to work with a devoted attitude, picking up the mantle with a fresh perspective from the Lord. But this was not without difficulty. One afternoon, weary from serving staff and guests, I walked into the nearby forest to pray. As I poured out my heart, the Lord's response caught me by surprise, and I gained a new outlook.

The Lord revealed that our ministry had a purpose: to provide warmth and shelter for traveling saints. And just as the physical walls of the base were being rebuilt, it was time for the mission's ministry of hospitality to be restructured. Hospitality was to be YWAM's forerunning ministry.

God has used hospitality tremendously. Hearts have been touched, melted, and saved. Hospitality has also played a significant role in bonding the YWAM family to our local and Christian communities and other missionary organizations.

We have been called by God to wave the flag of hospitality. We have been asked to minister to the saints and to refresh their hearts. The effectiveness of the ministry will be in direct proportion to the love, commitment, and servant attitude expressed by each of us.

As you read this book, consider how its suggestions and experiences can be used in your ministry. Although many of the stories describe YWAM experiences, practices, and structure, the principles can be adapted for any individual or ministry desiring to walk in the ministry of hospitality. Don't hesitate to "give a cool cup of water to someone who is thirsty. . . . The smallest act of giving or receiving makes you a true apprentice. You won't lose out on a thing" (Matt. 10:42 MSG).

chapter 1

a place to call home

TRULY I TELL YOU, ANYONE WHO GIVES YOU A CUP

OF WATER IN MY NAME BECAUSE YOU BELONG TO THE

MESSIAH WILL CERTAINLY NOT LOSE THEIR REWARD.

MARK 9:41

Having been involved in ministry for many years, I have lived in various places, from a one-room dwelling in Uganda to a gorgeous home with a beautiful view in Kona, Hawaii. Early in our marriage, my husband Arnold and I realized that "home is wherever we are together." We have had some interesting places to call home! But I've learned to make each home represent our family, and that has helped us settle in more quickly.

Each of us determines the atmosphere of our home. To me, a home is a place where God and peace reside. Those who dwell within its walls receive love and acceptance. Home is a place of shelter and retreat—a place where one can be refreshed and built up before going out to minister. Home is a place where friends are welcomed.

One of my family's favorite homes was a small European-style apartment in Switzerland where we lived when our children were young. Our living room was so tiny that when one visiting family sat with us, their boys' feet touched in the middle of the room when they sat across from each other on chairs. On one occasion, we hosted a banana-split party for twenty-five people. After being served an ice cream treat, each person sat in one room or another in the house. Our two oldest children, seven and eight at the time, hosted guests in their bedroom. The living room and kitchen were packed with bodies, and laughter rang throughout the house. We have great memories of rich fellowship and visits from friends during that six-year season of our lives.

I have come to realize that the goal and function of our home is to create a pleasant setting for ministry, family, friends, and new acquaintances. I ask myself, do people feel free to come to our door at any time? Do I make time for them when they visit?

Certain elements in our home are a priority: comfortable spots to sit, good lighting, and a warm atmosphere. More importantly, our home provides emotional comfort, safety, and freedom to be one's self. Still, physical beauty and eye appeal cannot be underestimated. A home should be an oasis filled with beauty—a clean and comfortable place filled with personal touches that reflect everyone who lives there. Children's artwork and creative projects can add unique touches of color and texture. And a gardener in the family, like my husband, can beautify outdoors.

People's thoughts often turn to those places where they have been brought in from the cold and given a seat by the fire to enjoy the people, the hugs, and the laughter they cherish. As we look into visitors' eyes and tell them how important they are to us, we are welcoming them into the home of our heart. We should always pay attention to details that make guests feel comfortable—the more relaxing the atmosphere, the easier it is to feel included.

After a two-week visit to our home, one of my favorite people wrote, "Thank you for an environment of trust and relaxation."

In another note, a relative said, "I genuinely felt welcomed and cared for—no fake hospitality here!" I am always glad to know that our home represents our hearts.

Opening your home in joyful hospitality builds bridges to those who need Jesus. In today's society, getting people together to fellowship, laugh, and develop friendships is essential. Our amazing God places no value on possessions. He doesn't pressure us to perform or require us to be sophisticated. Instead, he sees our hearts and understands us. Through his Holy Spirit, he uses us to help heal the broken and hurt spirits of those who need his love. Let your home be a place where this happens. People may forget what you said or what you did, but they will never forget how you made them feel.

Hospitality is linked to celebration. Celebrate being together! Share what you have; prepare your home and what you can offer artistically, and God will take care of the rest. His very nature is to give everything he has. God always provides if we invest what we have. Don't hold out and say you'll wait until you have more to give. Open your hand and give whatever you can, even a small amount. If our family had waited for a perfect, big home and necessary financial reserves, we would have never experienced the joy of extending hospitality.

In Matthew 25:34–40, Jesus explains that when we give food, drink, clothing, and personal care to others, we do it unto him. Our heavenly Father has made a way for us not only to minister to others but to serve him at the same time. Hospitality is to be exercised in our homes as a means of ministry to those in need.

When we are called to ministry, we quickly learn that our home belongs to the Lord and he will use it for his purposes, taking into account our personalities, gifts, and callings. If your home belongs to him, he will bring people to your door whom you least expect to see there. Jesus sat among the unclean, the leper, the prostitute, and the drunkard, and he may ask us to do the same. If we are his disciples, we must be open to receive the world and to love others as he did.

Homes play an important role in establishing a feeling of love, acceptance, and rich fellowship. When making new acquaintances, my first instinct is to bring them to our home. I like to flood our lives with friends and relationships in all their beauty and brokenness. Sometimes I caution myself against thinking that I must be in a place for at least three months to make it a home. Living in a temporary state and knowing that I am going to move on may bring up the question, what's the point? Yet there may be a very significant one.

We can touch lives everywhere we go. When my family served for four weeks at the YWAM ministry campus in Kona, our one room quickly became a hubbub of activity. During that time, God spoke specific precious promises to our kids through our guests. I often think how much we would have missed had we not welcomed others into our temporary home.

Hospitality may make some of us nervous. I have learned to be prepared for the unexpected with a special beverage, baked good, and a quick meal tucked away in my freezer or pantry. When guests arrive, I can spend time with them and not be busy with preparations. Having the ability to extend our dining table gives us the option of making room for one more. A rule in our home is that no dishes are washed until the guests are gone. That way our guests get our full attention. Hospitality is not something you turn on; it is a way of life, and not a frazzled one. Listen to God as he directs, and do only what he says to do—no more and no less. Invest whatever you have so that God can work his multiplication miracles. Jesus the servant is aware of our limitations and our capabilities to serve under pressure.

Treat your guests, anticipate their needs, and above all, make them feel comfortable. Some friendships are brief, but many blossom into rare gifts of beauty. I have special friendships with people all over the world, and many began with a simple act of hospitality.

Ministering as a family has always been a priority for Arnold and me. Our children, too, have played an active role in the hospitality ministry. When children live in a hospitable home, they imitate what is modeled. Greeting people at the door, taking coats, and finding conversation topics becomes natural. Our kids have grown up knowing that we want to bless people in our home, so they have been constantly involved in the serving. We have had the privilege of having godly men and women grace our doors and share a meal with us. Our kids love listening to the stories shared around the dinner table. I believe this has helped shape and form them into the people they are today. As guests in our home share their experiences, they become a great resource of ministry to our children.

Involve your kids in discussions of who to invite to your home, and how often. If the same people come too frequently, kids may become insecure and unsure of their own places in their parents' lives. However, repeat visitors can become important people to your children. I appreciate the adults who had a special interest in our kids. Because of those relationships, our three children have aunties and uncles all over the world, which is a blessing since we have never lived near our extended biological family. Our kids help plan events in our home, especially when they involve young people. The kids know "the latest" in food trends. Our children are older now, but the fond memories of tea parties, sleepovers, birthday parties, and dinner guests linger on.

For our family, successful parties depend on knowing our audience and accommodating our guests with appropriate food and enjoyable activities. Each celebration can be personalized. We often have African coworkers working with us, and since meat is enjoyed in their culture, I always serve it. When my husband's family visits, out come the board games because that's what they enjoy.

A simple supper can become a grand time from start to finish. Sitting across from one another at mealtime makes for a wonderful occasion. It gives people the opportunity to share thoughts and experiences in an atmosphere of trust and relaxation.

Mealtime conversation—talking and listening—is an art. Try to involve everyone, adults and children alike, in the conversation. Stimulate conversation with friendly debates, but avoid criticism, which causes most people to retreat and become quiet. This is particularly true with children. Opportunities for great conversation, fun, and laughter are as numerous as the types of foods we eat.

In a mysterious way, food is a form of communication. It is a part of the message Jesus revealed to us. The multiplication of loaves and fishes, the wedding feast miracle of turning water into wine, the offering of the bread and cup—all are powerful expressions of how Jesus used food to show us his ways.

I have sat at many tables in my lifetime. Some were in a setting of plenty, and others in poverty. At some I learned to give; at others I learned to receive. But at each table I learned that taking time to share the stories of our lives is as important as sharing food and shelter.

I've learned that good manners make others feel at ease. A greeting is always appropriate and important, even if it's a big smile where there is a language barrier. Always say thank you in some way to those who have served you. Observe and learn what is expected in various circumstances. For instance, I have learned to eat politely with my hands or, in another setting, to remove my shoes at a front door.

Manners are a lifetime gift we can pass on to our children as they learn the values we cherish. Yet teaching children manners on the spot is usually not a good idea. Before arriving at another home, try to prepare children for appropriate practices and customs. This helps them enter the situation with confidence and know what is expected of them.

In one Thai village we visited, our hosts were living on very limited resources, yet they showered us with hospitality, prepared a special meal, and offered small gifts to us. As we sat on a dirt floor, my children displayed gratefulness and good manners even though they had never before been served dog meat, which is a delicacy in that culture. We then enjoyed a beautiful afternoon of fellowship together.

Hospitality is a cool cup of water, a simple beverage, an attentive ear that will honor a stranger or a friend. In many parts of the world, serving a beverage is the same as extending friendship. In India, offering a cup of tea is a symbol of accepting and identifying with another person. Be it a corn drink in Latin America, a cup of tea in Asia, or a ginger drink in Africa, a beverage is an invitation to sit, stay awhile, share recent events, and be refreshed. Hospitality matters, and home is where it begins.

why hospitality matters: serving, loving, and giving

DON'T FORGET TO SHOW HOSPITALITY TO STRANGERS, FOR SOME WHO

HAVE DONE THIS HAVE ENTERTAINED ANGELS WITHOUT REALIZING IT!

HEBREWS 13:2 NLT

According to Webster's Dictionary, "To be hospitable is to be in a warm way and manner and to entertain with generous kindness." Hospitality involves sensitivity and availability. We want the people that God puts in our paths to feel they are welcome. This means that we need to emphasize the warmth and personal ways of our ministry. When we graciously welcome and receive our friends, family, fellow staff, and guest speakers, they are free to be and do their best. Hospitality is about giving, serving, and loving people. Our guests often return the blessing to us.

What I love most about the ministry of hospitality is that it was God's idea in the first place, and he gives us so much instruction through his Word. For the committed Christian, hospitality is a scriptural command, an obligation as well as a privilege. Hospitality is not just social protocol; it is a ministry close to the heart of God.

For some people, hospitality comes as naturally as breathing. Others must learn to be hospitable. But for all of us, the gift must be continually nurtured. We need the Holy Spirit to teach us how to be sensitive to one another's needs and how to best serve each guest.

Scripture is full of scenarios and examples of hospitality. In Romans 12:13, we are encouraged to "practice hospitality." Other scriptures elaborate on this verse, encouraging us to welcome people to our homes and minister to their practical needs.

The apostle Paul depended on the ministry of hospitality as he traveled. One of my favorite verses on hospitality is Romans 15:32: "so that I may come to you in joy by the will of God and find refreshing rest in your company" (NASB).

The Bible teaches that every activity of our lives is to be worship to God. Everything we do, we should do for him (1 Cor. 10:31).

According to Titus 1:8, a leader must be hospitable. My friend Darlene Cunningham understands this well. "A bonding takes place when you bring someone into your home and get to know them," Darlene says. "This transparency and generosity is characteristic of the conduct we need to have as leaders."

All that we have belongs to the Lord, and we are stewards, or caretakers, of it. Because of this, we are to have an attitude of sharing, realizing that as God blesses his children with material gifts and talents, we are to enjoy and share them. A giving heart is essential to hospitality.

Jesus, our example in ministry, displayed a giving heart as he identified with people in need. Without compromising truth, he became one with the people to whom he ministered. His acceptance and understanding were expressions of his deep compassion and concern for all people. He humbly associated with men and women of deep need and great sin, showing them the way to freedom and wholeness. As we follow his example, our service is extended not only out of compassion for others but also as a testimony to the Lord Jesus Christ.

Ultimately, people are important and significant because they are made in the image of God, not because of their occupations or beliefs. It is difficult to entirely separate a person from his role in society or what she believes, but God is more concerned about our relationships than the roles we fulfill. We must go beyond role-oriented relationships and share ourselves personally with people of all backgrounds.

In 1974 a missionary to Japan arrived unexpectedly at YWAM Lausanne in Switzerland. An associate of Billy Graham, he had arrived to help set up a conference. This man was extremely impressed by the warm welcome he received. His wife, hearing about his visit, assumed that he had received special treatment because he was a key figure in an international evangelism congress.

When the woman later joined her husband at the ministry, no one knew who she was. She was blessed to be welcomed in the same warm manner. Because of the hospitality she received, YWAM was invited to participate in two of the conferences that her husband was involved with.

"The ministry of hospitality opened the door," YWAM leader Joe Portale pointed out following the Japanese missionary's visit. Joe was reminded of Hebrews 13:2: "Do not neglect to show hospitality to strangers, for by this some have entertained angels without knowing it" (NASB).

Our world is filled with scarred, hurt people, and their needs will never be met unless we go beyond role-oriented relationships and share ourselves personally. To identify with a person in need is to follow the example of Jesus. We are to serve people not only out of compassion for them but also as a testimony to him. Our ministry should

- salute the value of the individual;
- affirm the uniqueness of other cultures;
- show honor;
- lay a basis for learning from past and future generations.

"When God's children are in need, you be the one to help them out. And get into the habit of inviting guests home for dinner or, if they need lodging, for the night" (Rom. 12:13 TLB). In essence, hospitality is holy because holiness is other-centered. It is looking beyond ourselves to show people they are valuable and worthwhile, while letting God express himself through us. Hospitality takes many forms, but the heart stays the same. The root of hospitality is giving value, acceptance, and love. This ignites the power to restore and refresh our guests.

Each one of us has a kingdom assignment. God invests in us so that we will invest in others and carry his heart to them. We know when we move in hospitality that we are living our lives the way God means for us to live them—in openness, sharing, and love. Are you given to hospitality?

Most of us have seen examples of what hospitality is not. Hospitality done right requires being authentic with who we are, creating an environment of refreshing peace and quiet, restoring souls, giving value, and anticipating needs. The attitude of a host should be, "You will not be in need as long as you are my guest." God wants to lavish his love on people. We want our guests to leave on a different level than when they arrived. As we give our guests value, love, and acceptance, they will be changed.

Here are a few quotes from notes left behind by guests in our home.

A friend from Holland: "Thank you so much for a wonderful stay at your home. I've really enjoyed it, although I missed home. It was so great to see the country where you live, so different from what we are used to. It was even greater to feel the love and hospitality, not artificial but real."

A friend from Singapore: "Thank you so much for making me feel so welcome in your home. Thank you for sharing so many things with me and the time that you've taken for us."

A friend from South Africa: "I was so relaxed in your home. You gave me an environment of trust and relaxation. I feel so refreshed."

These responses happen "just because" we go beyond ourselves and allow God to move through us.

HOSPITALITY VERSUS ENTERTAINING

Many people equate hospitality with entertaining, considering the two words to be synonymous. Hospitality can include entertaining, just as entertaining can involve hospitality. But there is a vast difference between the ageless concept of hospitality and our modern practices of entertaining. Historically, the rich did not share. Mansions weren't inviting, but tents were!

Hospitality implies welcoming people into one's home or environment for the purpose of meeting the guests' needs and making them comfortable. When we invite guests to participate in our personal lifestyle, whether for an hour or many days, we can expect God to do great things through us. Hospitality implies spontaneity. True hospitality doesn't make us feel pressured or worn out. Love transforms an event into true hospitality. Life sharing is not entertaining on our own strength. Hospitality is an art form that can be learned by making others feel welcome in our midst at any given time.

Entertaining, on the other hand, is done more to please or impress guests, often with a focus on food and social entertainment. Entertaining is easy—anyone, given the time and money, can impress a visitor. Yet entertaining can be a job rather than a joy; it can even be seen as an obligation.

While entertaining may be impersonal, without emotional involvement, a caring heart is crucial for the ministry of hospitality. It is impossible to be hospitable without involving the heart. When we do it to serve Jesus and others, hospitality takes on new meaning.

HOSPITALITY AS A MINISTRY

The ministry of hospitality is very close to the heart of God. When the Lord admonished us to practice hospitality, he knew what a blessing it would be to both host and guest. As God designed it, hospitality serves many purposes and has multiple results.

Just what does hospitality accomplish? It ministers to people and refreshes their hearts. It gives them rest and rejuvenation, allowing them to more effectively share the Lord with others. Hospitality makes newcomers feel welcome; the cordial, generous reception of guests draws them into a family atmosphere. It creates a safe place and says, "We value you." Hospitality provides free space where strangers can become friends. Hospitality is extended not to change people but to offer a place for that to happen.

Hospitality bonds people together, building relationships between individuals with varying similarities and differences. It opens doors that previously would not budge. Many deep friendships have developed between people who first got acquainted when one opened his or her heart in a gesture of hospitality.

As hospitable people, we need to be available and take the time. We must lay down personal desires, offering a place of rest or a listening ear. In doing this we create a cozy and warm atmosphere, no matter what the weather is like. Guests immediately realize when hospitality is valued, and they will return for more.

One day our Amsterdam hospitality team received a desperate call. A missionary couple was returning to Canada from Africa, where they served with a different mission organization. Upon arrival in Amsterdam, they had no place to stay and asked if they could spend the night at our ministry. It had been a busy day for me, and I didn't feel like receiving unexpected guests. But God spoke to me about welcoming them and preparing their room generously, with extra care. So I purchased beautiful flowers and some delicious Dutch food and made their room extra special. The couple arrived, and after I helped them settle in, they spent the weekend quietly and left a note of thanks when they departed.

Two years later, I was working in Canada at a different YWAM location. One of our speakers was the man who had been our unexpected visitor in Amsterdam. He stopped me at the door and said, "Debbie, I know you—were you our hostess in Amsterdam?" I said I was, and he told me how the hospitality of the room I'd prepared had ministered to him and his wife. At that time, they were going through personal hardship. The welcome, generosity, and honor they experienced when they entered the guest room in Amsterdam had truly blessed them. It had given them the courage to go home and meet with family and friends to share about their difficulties and discouragement.

Once again I thanked the Lord for his faithfulness in reminding me of the infinite value of hospitality. At the time the man came to speak at the school, one of the school leaders was questioning the value of money spent on hospitality. Then he heard the speaker's story of thankfulness and saw the flower bouquet of appreciation he brought me the next day. Suddenly there was a new understanding of our ministry, and I received an ample budget for the remainder of the school term. This is a story of double blessings. I gave of myself to bless unexpected visitors, and God honored that—even two years later—with an unexpected blessing in return.

Guests can sense if hospitality is not important, so a host's positive attitude toward guests is essential. Experts tell us that communication is 93 percent nonverbal, which means that if you are not at ease, your guests will not be either. Adopt the attitude that there is always room for one more. Remember, the spirit of hospitality is not in the perfect accommodation or feast—it is in the heart of the host.

As the heartbeat of any ministry or home, hospitality is a means of serving, loving, and giving. A core principle of practicing hospitality is to do it over and over. We may do this corporately or individually, but in either case we receive many blessings.

I experienced this personally while hosting conferences for YWAM International Leadership Teams at different locations. Each gathering required planning and logistics, many meals to cook and serve, and effort and hard work from several individuals. But there were also blessings as spiritually mature Christians came together with encouragement and prayer for the ministry as a whole and for individual YWAM ministries. The benefits we received from hosting were far greater than the effort we extended.

God's Word tells us that the Lord loves a cheerful giver. He wants us to give freely with no expectation of anything in return. Generosity with our time, energy, and money is a wise and worthwhile investment. It may not always be what we expect or desire, but God is faithful to give back to us. That is his heart: to bless those who give.

Hospitality is an offering to the Lord that seeks to minister, not impress. We should avoid the "my situation must be perfect" syndrome and avoid comparing our accommodations with others.

Just before my family returned to Lausanne for the rebuild in 1994, Darlene and I planned a hospitality seminar. The brochures announcing the seminar had already been distributed when we arrived, but to our dismay, we quickly discovered how limited the facilities were. The chalet was in shambles, with little space and very tight living quarters. Other buildings were in poor condition. Where would we hold the seminar?

We decided to use the small upstairs area of the Cunninghams' home for our meetings. The "upper room" was like the room where Jesus met with his disciples, and we had twelve "disciples" just like he did. (Earlier, I had prayed for twelve people to attend. The day before the seminar, eleven had registered. Then a woman from Egypt arrived and become the twelfth in the group.) Though rocks were falling from the ceiling, we were together, and God met us in a special way. Our prayer times were wonderful; one day we basked in the warmth of the Holy Spirit for three hours. Each participant was truly equipped and refreshed at the end of this seminar.

To this day, that hospitality seminar remains one of my favorites. The participants not only accepted our humble surroundings, but they felt privileged to be at our ministry during that restoration time. Each one of us was glad to be there.

Here are questions we all should consider:

To whom should we show hospitality? Essentially, anyone can be the recipient. Often it is members of the body of Christ who come our way to teach, learn, or stop to rest during their travels. Strangers may also appear at our doorstep, needing a place to spend the night or eat a meal. Or we may be approached by the poor and hungry who have no provisions.

How can we communicate God's love to these people? We express God's love by showing that we value our visitors and focusing our attention on them. Making eye contact is important, as is appropriate physical touch. A handshake or perhaps a touch on the shoulder will make a visitor feel welcome.

How can hospitality be an evangelism tool? Being hospitable accomplishes more than filling a stomach or providing a place to rest. Our openness and willingness to serve shows others how the body of Christ functions. Our example is the only way some people will come to know God. A relationship with Christ is relevant to today's society. It counteracts the isolation, fear, and loneliness that run rampant in our world.

Hospitality and friendship go hand in hand. But many Christians who feel that their time is wasted if not invested in specific religious activities have lost the art of friendship. Being a friend may involve listening to a neighbor's troubles, offering help, or assisting with a project. It may include participating in nonreligious activities of mutual interest, such as sporting events, hobbies, home maintenance, or yard work. Activities like these often lay a foundation for meaningful conversation. If we commit our time to the Lord, the Holy Spirit will, in his time, give opportunity to speak of spiritual things.

FIVE ELEMENTS OF HOSPITALITY

The elements needed for abundant hospitality are an open heart, an open home, generosity, creativity, and cultural sensitivity.

An open heart

An open heart is motivated by a love for people. Hospitality implies enjoyment. Our guests should feel that we care about them and want to spend time with them. Whether hospitality succeeds or fails depends on the host's attitude. If the host is not at ease, guests will not be either.

To give our guests the feeling that we want to serve them, we must start by being receptive to those we host. We are doing this for God, and we can trust that he is putting people into our lives. We know that he will help us as we turn to him. He gives us willingness to serve and even softens our hearts toward those who may be challenging guests.

An open home

A home, room, or ministry location open to guests is a place where guests may be refreshed and encouraged. It is the surrounding in which guests will bond with the host individual, family, or community. Our doors must be wide open. Over the years, many opportunities for hospitality have opened to us as a mission. We need to be quick to say yes to accommodate others.

The key word here is *open.* There is an old saying: "It is not the house but the people in it that make a home." Hospitality is not dependent upon environment or possessions. Just equipping a house does not necessarily make it a home where guests and strangers feel at ease and welcome. I have yet to shake hands with a friendly couch or said, "How do you do?" to a polished dining table. The attitude of the host is the keynote on which hospitality sings.

When Arnold and I take our family on mission trips, we tell the kids it's like a long camping trip where we live in one room instead of a tent. One year we traveled to South Africa, where Arnold was on staff at a training development school. We lived in one room, furnished with a plastic table and chairs and always open to visiting staff and students. We even had a birthday party there. It was a wonderful experience, inviting people into our little home. We often think that we need a large space to host visitors, but small rooms work too. Hospitality should be spontaneous and remain in our hearts wherever we are. Where there is room in the heart, there is room in the home.

Generosity

Being generous with our time and resources is a gift to others. Even a cup of cold water in Jesus' name can be a blessing. There have been times where my family, suffering from thirst in foreign countries, received welcome relief from a cup of cold water.

Hospitality need not be a financial burden. As we practice generosity, something special happens. It is our choice to be generous, but by refusing to give, we miss opportunities for blessing.

When my husband and I were newlyweds, we served in YWAM Uganda. My friend Monica invited us to her home. To our delight, the house was a typical African hut. We had a wonderful afternoon sharing with Monica's extended family. We were treated like royalty, as if Arnold and I were the king and queen.

When we arrived, we noticed a few chickens running around. Four hours later we sat down to the table and were served cooked chicken. (I now noticed that I didn't hear the chickens outdoors anymore.) Monica told us that her parents had cooked their last chickens for us. They truly served a meal straight from their hearts.

Arnold and I were humbled by the generosity of this family. When we left, they gave us an African gift. They felt honored to have had us in their home, and we felt privileged to have been there.

This lesson was first learned during my early days with YWAM when I was still single. I was preparing to host my small group at our ministry location in Hawaii and felt that the Lord had impressed me to serve a special treat—Kona coffee ice cream. I knew it would take my last three dollars, but I was sure it was the right thing to do. I bought the ice cream and came home with twenty-five cents in my pocket, not knowing where my next dollar would come from. The next day, a generous check unexpectedly arrived from one of my dear aunts. It was as if God had said, "I'll meet you for the day. As long as you are being hospitable and giving from your heart, I will meet you."

Creativity

Creativity is a beautiful expression of our Creator. It is the ability to think beyond the norm, to glorify and reflect God. We all express creativity in different ways because we're all different.

When I lived in Uganda, gardenias, ground nuts, and banana bark became my staples for hospitality. It was always pleasing when I laid out my refreshments using resources available. Often one person's creativity complements another's, and the end product can be truly unique. Allow yourself the time and effort to creatively welcome your guests. There is great satisfaction in making something out of nothing.

Sharing creativity has made working with my friend Darlene Cunningham very special to me for all these years. We feed off each other's creativity. We both tend to work with "classic" taste in mind. Darlene comes up with an idea, and I often carry it out for her. It has been a wonderful time of discovering how we can work together as we complement each other.

Cultural sensitivity

Making room in our hearts for people from all cultures requires sensitivity. The spirit of hospitality is the same no matter where we are or where we are from, but we often do things differently, and we must try to make things culturally appropriate.

We miss out on the international aspect of our world and communities by dwelling on the challenges of understanding different cultures. Look at it as a great adventure to learn about different people and areas of the world; it is a blessing to experience. And share your culture with your guests! It's a gift from the Father for visitors to experience authentic Thai food, a traditional Hawaiian luau, or a South African *braai* (barbeque).

WHEN IT'S OKAY TO SAY NO

Keep your eyes open for opportunities to extend hospitality. But watch that the enemy doesn't sidetrack you from what the Lord wants you to do. We can become weary with well-doing, and usually our fatigue shows through. At times it is all right to say no to requests for hospitality. One person can't be everything to everyone, and our ministries cannot meet every need.

YWAM teacher and University of the Nations provost Tom Bloomer describes hospitality ministers as "gatekeepers," a role to be taken seriously. It is up to a hospitality team to determine if a potential guest should be accepted or denied. A guest can do a great deal of good or a great deal of harm to a community or family. The generosity of hospitable people can be abused, and we must be aware of that. Do not encourage a selfish person to continue to be selfish. Don't give in to pressure or base your decision on human sympathy. It is true that the Lord sends most of our guests, but the devil can send people too.

Rely on the Holy Spirit for guidance. He will instruct you about which people to invite and include, which people to specifically pray over, and when to do nothing at all. If you hesitate about a request, or if you don't feel right about it or just aren't sure, go to the Lord about it. Pray about each request and each proposed guest list. God may lead you to refuse a request because he has a better idea or a more appropriate place for a visitor to be received at that time.

The first morning I worked in hospitality at YWAM Heidebeek in the Netherlands, the Lord impressed on me that I needed to be alert that day. The day was full of busyness with many different situations. That evening, three backpackers walked onto the base and asked if we could accommodate them. My heart was open, but my spirit didn't feel peaceful about allowing them to stay. I recommended the youth hostel in town and helped the travelers get there safely.

I often wondered why God didn't want those backpackers to stay with us, but I was faithful to respond to the check in my spirit. I believe the Lord wanted me to be flexible enough to say no in response to his prompting. Since then, I have made a habit of "checking in" with the Lord to ask him if our ministry is the best place for each person to stay. Sometimes it isn't.

Be open not only to scheduled but also spontaneous hospitality. Impromptu situations may come up unexpectedly, leaving little or no time to organize and plan. When that happens, sit down, relax, and think of options and possibilities. Gather your ideas together and come up with a plan. For starters, keep it simple and go from there. Try to avoid being rushed. When you are totally surprised by an unannounced or early arriving guest, offer a snack and beverage to be enjoyed while you retreat and put together a plan.

Our hearts should always be ready to receive, honor, and accommodate unexpected guests. Greet them with joy and warmth even if two more for dinner will throw off your carefully planned table settings. People are more important than pretty tables. Christ was our example in this—didn't he always have food and room for one (not to mention five thousand) more?

Sometimes we get tired of serving. But let's remember at these times to run to Jesus for refreshment and a refill of his strength and joy in serving. The Lord will renew us; it's a promise he made. It's not wrong to express our needs to him or to ask for encouragement to keep going. Here is a sampling of what God's Word says about hospitality.

Cheerfully share your home with those who need a meal or a place to stay for the night. God has given each of you some special abilities; be sure to use them to help each other, passing on to others God's many kinds of blessings.

1 Peter 4:9–10 TLB

Don't forget to be kind to strangers, for some who have done this have entertained angels without realizing it!

Hebrews 13:2 TLB

Do nothing from selfishness or empty conceit, but with humility of mind, regard one another as more important than yourselves; do not merely look out for your own personal interests, but also for the interests of others.

Philippians 2:3–4 NASB

And let us not get tired of doing what is right, for after a while we will reap a harvest of blessing if we don't get discouraged and give up. That's why whenever we can we should always be kind to everyone, and especially to our Christian brothers.

Galatians 6:9–10 TLB

An overseer, then, must be above reproach, the husband of one wife, temperate, prudent, respectable, hospitable, able to teach.

1 Timothy 3:2 NASB

Do not withhold good from those to whom it is due, when it is in your power to do it.

Proverbs 3:27 NASB

For whoever gives you a cup of water to drink because of your name as followers of Christ, truly I say to you, he will not lose his reward.

Mark 9:41 NASB

Then Jesus said to his host, "When you give a luncheon or dinner, do not invite your friends, your brothers or sisters, your relatives, or your rich neighbors; if you do, they may invite you back and so you will be repaid. But when you give a banquet, invite the poor, the crippled, the lame, the blind.

Luke 14:12–13

Conduct yourselves with wisdom toward outsiders, making the most of the opportunity.

Colossians 4:5 NASB

*To what can I compare this generation? They are like children
sitting in the marketplaces and calling out to others.*

Matthew 11:16

*But they urged him strongly, "Stay with us, for it is
nearly evening; the day is almost over."*

Luke 24:29

Hospitality is the silver thread that connects other parts of ministry. In 1 Timothy 3:2, it's clear that hospitality is essential for Christian leaders. As we teach and model hospitality, others will learn from our example. Something special is imparted when leaders open their homes and hearts. If leaders of each ministry set the precedent, then others will follow.

getting started: how-to basics from the heart

IN RESPONSE TO ALL HE HAS DONE FOR US, LET US

OUTDO EACH OTHER IN BEING HELPFUL AND KIND

TO EACH OTHER AND IN DOING GOOD.

HEBREWS 10:24 TLB

What makes an excellent host or hostess? The most vital characteristic is a desire to serve. With that attitude, all other details will fall into place. It is not what things you have to offer but the offering of your heart that makes hospitality successful. What a joy it is for guests to be greeted warmly by a host or hostess who has prepared both heart and home in anticipation of their arrival.

Some people seem to be born hospitable. Usually they have natural tendencies toward nurturing and caring for others. Their families may have had open homes with guests coming and going. For others, hospitality is more of a challenge. It doesn't come naturally and may not have been modeled for them. Or they may have had such excellent role models that they feel they could never measure up.

Whether we were born into it or work hard at it, any of us can be hospitable. As a biblical mandate, it is a skill that can be learned and a way of life to which we can adapt. What's important here are a desire to serve and a willingness to learn and stretch ourselves.

Hospitality is one of my spiritual gifts; God made me this way. I also grew up in a family where hospitality was valued and a part of everyday life. When I joined YWAM, I moved easily into the hospitality ministry and participated in its growth. Many men and women who had little or no prior experience in hospitality have assisted me.

Some key steps will help us grow in learning hospitality. First, develop a love relationship with God. You will naturally ascend to a new level of worship and praise. Learn to express your gratitude to him; thank him daily! Allow him to minister in your heart. Believe what he says about you, and believe his affirmations that come through others.

As you learn to understand, accept, and love yourself, you will be able to extend more of yourself in service to others. Serving is showing love by meeting practical and spiritual needs. If you lose sight of this, then the work becomes routine. Find joy in giving of yourself to bless others. Just as the Lord served those around him, serving others is the key to fulfillment.

There are numerous qualities that are assets to being a host. Alertness to specific needs and likes or dislikes of guests helps, as do discernment of practical needs and motivation to meet them quickly. We should be able to serve without hovering. Generosity is a helpful quality, as we are often asked to share what little we have to feed or house others. Spontaneity and flexibility to deal with interruptions, distractions, and changes of plans are musts. A sense of humor definitely helps!

On one occasion, just before a group of staff members was to move from Hawaii to Switzerland, Loren and Darlene Cunningham hosted a group of Asian businessmen for two weeks. The visitors were in Kona to hear messages about family, business, and other pertinent issues. The hospitality team had fun creatively preparing a variety of American dishes. One day we harvested fish from our aquaculture center's pond and barbecued for eighty people on the Cunninghams' lanai. Another time, we set up a sunset picnic on the beach.

For many of us it seemed like an inconvenient time for hospitality, as our hearts were ready for the move to Switzerland. But we gave it our all and ended up having a lot of fun preparing meals for our visitors. Our flexibility allowed us to be part of a wonderful week.

Be willing to take responsibility for whatever tasks must be done (even the dreary ones) and to serve in the background without fanfare or recognition. Be faithful in the mundane as well as the exciting, and know how to work quietly and obscurely, doing tasks that only the Lord may witness. Do not expect your deeds to be noticed by others, but be willing to allow the Lord to pat you on the back. He won't overlook your acts of service.

It takes physical and emotional stamina to wear so many hats and fulfill so many jobs. Fortunately, we have at our disposal a never-ending supply of the joy of the Lord, a thankful heart, and a willing spirit—all of which cover personal deficiencies and allow us to work beyond them. God has creative alternatives for challenging situations.

As a follower of Christ, be people-oriented. You can't be self-conscious and God-conscious at the same time. Trust the Lord when he surprises you with guests you wouldn't have chosen. He knows who needs your hospitality and when it's time to enlarge your tent. Learn to appreciate every visitor and to express the genuine value of his or her visit. Each of us represents the Lord as well as our ministry. If guests are new Christians or new to a church or ministry, their impressions of us will affect their impressions of God, and they will notice how we represent him.

Hospitality involves faithfulness with whatever gifts you have been given, which will complement the talents and skills of others. Be willing to accept help from others who have different gifts. Teamwork is effective and often required to handle the number of guests that will come your way.

If you're in a church or ministry, learn to be a part of a hospitality team. Work within the boundaries of your calling, without apologies for your shortcomings. Don't compare yourself to others, but recognize that we all have different styles. Don't try to adopt someone else's anointing; instead, invite that person to help you. Remain teachable so you can learn from others. Be open to new ideas and fresh input, which will enrich your own life and the lives of the guests you serve.

Even the roots of YWAM hospitality involved learning from others. Early on, our hospitality hostesses visited the Evangelical Sisterhood of Mary in Darmstadt, Germany. The Sisters had an incredible ministry and were eager to share with us. Our representatives observed the Sisters in action and learned at their sides. They came back with new and fresh ideas for hospitality at a large mission like ours.

Share what you do well, but also share your weaknesses. Work alongside people who can learn from you and from whom you can learn. Inspire and encourage one another in your areas of giftedness.

As you minister, it is crucial to know how you react under pressure. Do you buzz with activity? Stop? Withdraw? Do you explode with a temper or in tears? Once we recognize our reactions to situations, we can learn to control ourselves. Under pressure, it is often best to sit down and think in a private place. Be willing to be spontaneous, but know your limits. Discern what fits into your schedule and sphere of capabilities.

The people who pass through your home or church are very important to someone, including Jesus. Make each person feel valued and special. Nurture the art of conversation and learn something new about each guest. Ask questions and be interested in the answers. Find out what will make that person comfortable during the visit. Develop an attitude of godly love for your guests and a desire to take good care of them. Treat each visitor as you would treat Jesus.

As a host, you may become aware of personal or private matters in the lives of your guests. Use discretion as you handle this knowledge. Natural curiosity can be used for the wrong reasons. Use the information only to serve and minister to your guests. Personal information should not be shared unless someone else in the hospitality team needs to know. In any case, personal facts should not leave the hospitality department unless it is a matter for the ministry leader to handle. Be trustworthy in all situations.

If you have inconvenienced someone, give a complete apology. Begin by saying, "I'm really sorry; I know this has been uncomfortable for you." You may want to offer valid reasons for the inconvenience, but do not become defensive as you explain the circumstances.

As a guest, I've always enjoyed being greeted by hosts wearing national costumes (in Uganda and Indonesia). Costumes are not essential, of course, but personal hygiene is. When we look neat and clean, we represent ourselves well. This does not mean we have to wear the latest fashions. Our outward appearance is important to God as well as our inner beauty and character. I do not believe he wants us going around looking dowdy or unkempt. We are to be his witnesses to the world. Good grooming needs to be an important part of our morning routine as we prepare to meet the day with its many activities. We will see and meet people everywhere we go. It is vital to set a good standard of appearance.

Naturalness and godliness go hand in hand. When God has done a work in our lives, we can be transparent and at ease. We may have moments of doubt concerning our influence and worth, but with God's hand on our lives, our ministry can be a significant one. God has asked us to be hospitable hosts, molders of men and women. What a responsibility and privilege!

I was once part of a very busy hospitality team that was hosting a big leaders' conference. As our team was setting out the refreshments at the back of the meeting room, my attention immediately went to the speaker, who was speaking on the love of God. She said that God loves to lavish us with gifts and that we need to ask him with faith in our hearts for the gifts we'd like to have. I was challenged when the speaker invited us to pray for a specific gift from our intimate God. I had never done this before.

I must admit I was weary from a full day of serving. As I looked down at my hands before I prayed, I realized I had no jewelry on. So in faith I said, "God, I would love a pretty ring, and you know I love fresh flowers." To this day I will never forget the faith I felt in my heart with that prayer.

Out of God's great intimate love for me came answers to my prayer. When I returned to my room that evening to fall into bed, a huge bouquet of peach roses was beside it. No one knew I had prayed for flowers! One of my friends had been prompted by the Lord to give me the beautiful bouquet. I enjoyed them so much—a constant reminder of God's love to me.

The day the flowers died, God answered again. It was three weeks later, and an acquaintance I hardly knew surprised me at my door and wanted to take me to lunch. She shared that God woke her up and told her to bring me a gift. Out of obedience she had driven for two hours and arrived at my door with a gift. We went out to lunch— one of my favorite things to do—and I told her the story of my prayer of faith and how God shared his love with me through the flowers. My companion smiled and said that she felt she was to give me her grandmother's wedding ring. I couldn't believe what I heard. Her gift to me was a gorgeous diamond ring that perfectly fit my finger. It was quite a testimony to both of us of God's amazing, intimate love.

I am so glad I was serving that evening at the conference. Even though I felt weary, God taught me a lesson that I will never forget. My faith grew enormously. God loves to show himself through people by giving gifts and displaying his intimacy and generosity to us.

MAKE A LASTING FIRST IMPRESSION

We've all heard the saying "You don't get a second chance to make a first impression." This is quite true. It's important to make first impressions favorable ones. Here are some ideas.

- Shake hands in greeting whenever it seems a natural and easy gesture.
- Greet others with a smile that has warmth as well as width.
- Don't be afraid to laugh.
- Be outgoing—someone who is interested in other people and in the things that happen to them.
- Listen courteously whether the conversation interests you or not.
- Choose your confidantes with care, refraining from sharing troubles with a casual acquaintance.
- Show by your eye contact, questions, and comments that you are listening with your ears and mind.

CHECK YOUR ATTITUDE

Attitude shapes our thinking. Here are points to ponder for developing a healthy one.

- Have I completed my responsibilities? Have I gone the extra mile? 1 Corinthians 15:58, Hebrews 6:10
- Am I on time for activities? Ecclesiastes 3:1
- Do I cooperate with others? Philippians 2:2
- Do I respond positively, or do I grumble and complain when asked to do something? Philippians 2:14, 15
- Do I think before I speak? James 1:19, 20
- Is my appearance neat? 1 Corinthians 14:40
- Do I honor and pray for those over me? 1 Timothy 2:1, 2
- Does my behavior reflect control in difficult situations? Galatians 5:24, 25
- Do my conversation and actions edify others? Ephesians 4:29

leading your team

AND LET US NOT GET TIRED OF DOING WHAT IS RIGHT. FOR

AFTER A WHILE WE WILL REAP A HARVEST OF BLESSING

IF WE DON'T GET DISCOURAGED AND GIVE UP. THAT'S

WHY WHENEVER WE CAN WE SHOULD ALWAYS BE KIND TO

EVERYONE, AND ESPECIALLY TO OUR CHRISTIAN BROTHERS.

GALATIANS 6:9–10 TLB

Everyone appreciates a leader who manages well. There are many duties for which a hospitality ministry is responsible. These include preparing for, receiving, and hosting guests; purchasing hospitality supplies; directing ministry tours; creating and maintaining a community resource center; housekeeping of common areas of facilities; recognizing celebrations and accomplishments of coworkers; and organizing special events. These responsibilities will vary with the character and focus of your ministry location.

All of these procedures and the team of people who carry them out will be under the oversight of the hospitality team leader. This position is people oriented, not activity oriented. As a team leader, you will be required to carry out many activities, but it is people (you and your staff) who perform the tasks, and people (your guests) who receive your hospitality. Learn to manage your team well. Believe in each person and in the qualities each one brings to the team.

Delegating tasks is essential. Learn about your own and each team member's strengths and weaknesses. Workshops, brainstorming, and even personality tests will be helpful in identifying these things. Affirm and encourage your team in their areas of skill, and stimulate the development of their gifts by giving opportunity and assistance.

Determine how each person on your team responds to pressure. Many people "go with the flow," but others react with one of two extremes. There are the "buzzers" who are aware that something must be done. They respond with motion and activity. They may not accomplish much, but there is a lot of activity! The "paralyzed" person shuts down under pressure. This person can't think or act, and doesn't know what to do. For each type, manageable and creative steps help us get through a stressful period.

As you get to know your team members, you will know how to delegate responsibility in high-pressure circumstances. Who would be the best host or hostess for this situation? Who should be removed from it? Watch out for your team, and cover them when necessary. Manage the team's time in such a way that the workload is shared. Don't ask anyone to do a task that you yourself would not do.

Have regular times for team discussion, communication, scheduling, Bible study, and prayer. Group goal setting and sharing of ideas help develop and maintain a team spirit and group ownership of responsibilities. Include prayer for each other, your team, the community, and your guests. Develop a strong team of people who can work well together and trust one another.

Have an agenda and a plan for yourself and your hospitality team. Set daily, weekly, monthly, and annual goals for your ministry, while being flexible about changes. A good schedule is adaptable; don't forget that people are more important than things, events, or schedules. Prepare schedules that allow for required tasks plus extra time. Always leave time for the unexpected; never allow just one hour to do an hour's work. You never know what might happen during that hour. Your schedule is just a tool, not a rule.

Plan according to your energy level and that of those you work with. Be diligent to take time off when you need it, and encourage your team members to do the same. Don't hesitate to put a "Do Not Disturb" sign on your office door when you need uninterrupted time to plan or prepare. Do what you can to prevent burnout instead of dealing with it after it happens. Hospitality can be a highly stressful responsibility, and pressure can mount up quickly. Be aware of how your team members handle pressure, and know when they've had enough.

While providing hospitality, it is important to keep the area's culture and heritage alive and be open to other ideas and concepts that will improve efficiency. Each member of your team will come with fresh ideas and different ways of doing things. Be thankful for those improvements you discover together. Have a flexible spirit, and remember that an adventurous life can be exciting and rich.

While working in Holland, I was asked to lead hospitality for the GO Festival—a large missions youth conference—in Randers, Denmark. One of my hospitality team members was especially stressed by this project. One day I asked her if she was okay, and she burst into tears. The pressure had gotten the best of her, and she needed refreshment. I suggested that she go for a walk or rest for a couple of hours. Those were wonderful hours for both of us. The team member returned feeling renewed and revitalized, with a new perspective, and she was much more effective for the rest of the festival. In her two-hour absence, I filled in for her and was able to serve her in a special way.

As a team leader, you will have some pastoral responsibilities. God will use you to speak into the lives of your team members. Learn to communicate truth with kindness, respond to challenges with gentle answers, and request changes with the best interest of others in mind.

Affirm your staff members as a way to build team spirit and minimize misunderstandings. Be aware that affirmation is not manipulation, false flattery, or patronization; it is telling others what they do well. Use words to build up, not tear down. Compliments go a long way to ease tension, mend relationships, and heal wounded spirits. I remember one particular event that was an especially glorious time. Our team leader released us, trusted our teaching, and wrote daily words of encouragement to her team members by putting notes in our mailboxes. As a result, we soared as a team.

Recognize your hospitality team members' birthdays and other special occasions. Be loyal to your team members, stamping out little fires and ending petty arguments.

CREATIVE TEAMWORK

Creativity is a gift from God. Become familiar with the creative abilities and styles of your hospitality team. Hobbies and crafts come in very handy. Together we can make great things happen.

Varying personal styles create a smorgasbord of options for planning events and decorating. Members of your team may have a wide range of style preferences, anywhere from modern to traditional—so you'll have a great combination of styles to work with. The most important factor to remember is to be culturally appropriate for your location.

THE HOSPITALITY BUDGET

Budgeting can be a challenge for hospitality ministries, especially if it is not recognized as an important value. Think through the following principles and adopt those that will work in your situation. When setting a budget, it is helpful to define the responsibilities of the ministry team. You may come across many gray areas that should be discussed. In a ministry setting there may be money available from the general funds and also from specific budgets. As an example, the budget for an individual course may cover its own functions and its speakers' expenses, while the ministry covers general hospitality. Each ministry will deal with this differently. Become familiar with the policies of yours.

Work priorities into the budget, taking care of essentials first. It is poor stewardship to go beyond the budget, but make note of "extras" you would like to purchase if surplus funds become available. It is helpful to keep a small notebook with you at all times. You can jot down ideas or thoughts or note availability or pricing of certain items you see while shopping. I love to check off needed items as the Lord provides for them.

Each ministry has a different policy about charging guests for accommodations. Some charge a set fee, some charge nothing, and others request a donation to help cover expenses. In YWAM, many bases offer the first few days free and then suggest a donation amount. Some bases offer free hospitality to family of staff members but request a donation from other visitors. Teams visiting from other bases or ministries may have funds in their budget for these expenses and will be happy to pay for accommodations.

I consider YWAM a ministry, not a hotel. We can trust our Father to provide for us. I have worked in places that have sometimes charged a fee and not charged at other times. However, I saw a lot more money come into the hospitality department when we did not charge.

While rebuilding YWAM Lausanne, we were in dire financial need. Yet I felt that we weren't to charge our guests. Those first years, we received incredible amounts of money through hospitality. Guests staying with us knew that it cost something for us to host them. By not setting an amount, we freed the guests to ask the Lord how much to give, which was often much more than the amount we would have charged. One of my favorite testimonies was when a student's family came to visit over the Christmas holidays. The whole base enjoyed this family and embraced them. Upon leaving, they presented us with a check for several thousand dollars.

If we have prayed that our guests would come, we should receive them without expectation of payment. They have come to our ministry for a reason. This is especially true for parents and family of staff members. Having generously given up a child or sibling to ministry service, these guests have already given much.

DEALING WITH COMPLAINTS

How should criticism be handled? If one comes into your midst with a critical spirit, be gracious, responding with love of Jesus. Set aside any defensive feelings, and make your words be "apples of gold in settings of silver" (Prov. 25:11).

We don't have to receive everything that people tell us. However, we should listen and determine why a complaint is expressed. When we have been accused, our natural tendency is to point a finger back. But we must run to Jesus first. We need to take a deep breath, pull back, and ask Jesus to teach us and help us remember that in every criticism there is a nugget of truth. We can learn from a criticism and ask the Lord what to do with it.

In any case, remember that the hospitality department often serves as the public relations department of a ministry. Have information about your ministry and its mission readily available to share with visitors and to answer questions. Keep an ear open for complaints about your ministry. Perhaps you can tell the other side of the story or help explain why things are the way they are. It is not your responsibility to defend the ministry or its values. Offer to set up a meeting with a leader, if needed.

HOSPITALITY SUPPLIES TO HAVE ON HAND

This is an exhaustive list of supplies, and I have never seen a ministry that has all of them! If this list is overwhelming for your situation, take stock of the supplies that would enhance your hospitality ministry. Start with what is available locally, and supplement with items that may be brought from other places. As your ministry builds and you continue to be good stewards, God will supply you with the elements that are necessary and relevant in the culture you serve.

Event supplies

- Tablecloths of different colors and sizes
- Napkins: cloth and paper
- A set of dishes with cutlery
- Drinking glasses
- Trays of various sizes and shapes
- Small containers
- Serving dishes and trays
- Paper and/or plastic cups, paper plates, and plastic cutlery
- Baking pans for cookies, cakes, and muffins
- Birthday candles and matches
- Communion supplies: juice, crackers, cups or goblet
- Flower vases of different sizes
- Punch bowl and/or pitchers
- Thermal containers for coffee or hot water
- Coffee pots that are transportable (30- and 60-cup pots work well)
- Equipment for cultural specialties (in Switzerland we used fondue pots and raclette or table-top grills)
- Recipes and ingredients for local dishes

Food supplies

- Coffees and teas, cream, and sugar
- Cookies or small items that are quick and easy to serve
- Fruit and snack items
- Baking ingredients and recipes that are failproof

Guest room supplies and equipment

- Cleaning supplies
- Toiletries to supply room baskets
- Laundry baskets
- Matching sets of bed linens
- Matching sets of towels and washcloths
- Batteries for alarm clocks and other electronic gadgets
- Light bulbs
- Iron and ironing board
- Hangers
- Card-making supplies: papers, markers, stickers, scissors, and paints
- Variety of containers for welcome baskets and for serving food

communicating effectively

LIKE APPLES OF GOLD IN SETTINGS OF SILVER

IS A WORD SPOKEN IN RIGHT CIRCUMSTANCES.

PROVERBS 25:11 NASB

Communication is a major part of each person's role in hospitality. Communication with our guests occurs before, during, and after their visits. Each time we speak or write to a potential guest, we share a part of our ministry and ourselves. In a team, church, or family situation, each person is a representative of that group, expressing information and values through words and actions.

Effective communication makes people feel valuable. When we see people through God's eyes, we can be authentic, and people are drawn to Jesus. How we communicate with guests depends on several factors. Who are we welcoming? Is it a friend? An acquaintance? Age, cultural background, title, gender, purpose of visit, and length of stay all affect our communication. Ask yourself, would I feel welcome?

WHAT IS COMMUNICATION?

Much more than the exchange of words, communication involves the transmission and reception of ideas, feelings, and attitudes. Although we may think of communication mostly in terms of verbal expression, only 7 percent of a message is carried by words. The rest is communicated nonverbally through word choices, facial expressions, posture, and appearance.

Eye contact is important. In most cultures it is all right to connect eye to eye. With your eyes, you say to your guest, "I want to know you." Be attentive to the other person's side of the conversation. If you have a divergent mind or are easily distracted, it takes discipline to be engaged in a good conversation.

God has high ideals for our communication standards. Choose edifying, life-giving words over discouraging ones. In a conflict, lean forward with your heart and be open to both sides of the story.

Listening is as much a part of communication as speaking. Although talking comes naturally to many people, being a good listener is often the result of much practice and self-control. It is worth the effort to become a good listener, as sometimes a listening ear is just what a person needs. As a host, part of your job is to listen to people and learn about their interests, needs, and challenges. If listening is difficult, try to focus on the main point the speaker is making. Ask questions or redirect the conversation. Maintain eye contact and appear to be interested, even if you are not.

Conversation is an art that can be learned, and practice makes for improvements. Several factors contribute to successful and pleasing conversation. Words, of course, are important. Facial expressions, body language, and posture also say a lot. Verbal conversation can be read by the tone, speed, and volume of a voice. The tone should always match nonverbal cues; if in doubt, people usually trust and believe what is expressed nonverbally rather than the words spoken. Physical contact should be culturally appropriate, which may mean a handshake in one country and a kiss on the cheek in another. Warmth, smiles, and good humor are always fitting.

THE ART OF CONVERSATION

Upon arrival, a guest may not be in the mood for much conversation. Travel weariness, jet lag, language barriers, cultural differences, or even fear of strangers may affect the flow of conversation. Be careful not to use your hosting role to meet your own needs for fellowship. Don't push a guest to chat if he or she doesn't seem interested. Make an effort to discover any immediate practical needs you might meet. Then let the guest rest awhile.

During a guest's stay, you may have more opportunities for conversation. Ask more questions about your guest's life, work, family, and opinions on relevant topics. But be sensitive if he or she does not want to discuss a particular subject. Become an expert at rescuing awkward situations by changing the topic or redirecting the conversation. In general, avoid talk about money, health, controversial topics, gossip, or depressing subjects.

Silence is also a part of communication. Often you will be told about individual needs that are to be kept confidential. On the other hand, if you are told unnecessary details, don't dwell on them.

Use discretion in your conversations with guests. If you have disagreements, decide if it is appropriate or necessary to debate. Try to read into the situation and discern where your guest is coming from. It is better to be kind than right.

No matter how much planning you do, challenges may arise. You are on the Lord's assignment, so ask him for help in handling difficult situations. Don't make a bigger deal out of a situation than necessary, but work through any problems.

James 3:17 offers guidelines for conversations: pure, peaceable, gentle, reasonable, full of mercy and good fruit, unwavering, and without hypocrisy. Use discretion and integrity concerning what you see or hear in a situation. Poor communication or misinterpretation of a conversation can quickly turn into gossip. Be careful how you pass on information. Meditate on Psalm 141:3: "Set a guard, O LORD, over my mouth; keep watch over the door of my lips" (NASB).

CROSS-CULTURAL COMMUNICATION

We can easily have misunderstandings by not being sensitive to how different cultures communicate. In ages past, communication evolved similarly in areas of like climates. In my work with international students, I've learned that being aware of a person's climate helps us understand his or her frame of reference.

Those coming from colder climates value accuracy and have the ability to say what they really mean. Their yes means yes and their no means no. Time is valued, and as a result, their questions and answers may be short and to the point, showing respect to others in the conversation.

In warmer climates, a feel-good atmosphere is enjoyed. People go to great lengths to avoid offending or embarrassing others. A yes may not be an answer to your question. It can take a while to get to the point. In some cultures three invitations are expected before one will be accepted. I have some Asian friends who will not come over for fellowship until a third invitation. So keep asking.

EXTENDING INVITATIONS

A guest's first impression of you or your organization may come through your invitation. Make it a warm and loving one that clearly expresses the spirit of hospitality. Even if your first contact is through writing, e-mail, or a phone call, a smile can show through your words and voice. Make sure your message sounds friendly.

RESPONDING TO REQUESTS

When potential guests initiate a request to come for a visit, it may or may not be convenient for you or fit into your schedule. Be open to compromise. Work out a solution to any conflict or scheduling problem. Be clear and concise with your acceptance or refusal. How you respond is just as important as the answer you give.

RECEIVING GUESTS AND MAKING INTRODUCTIONS

Be physically, spiritually, and emotionally prepared to greet your visitor. There are two ways to view the arrival of a guest: "Oh no, not another one!" or "Praise the Lord—another visitor sent our way!" Your attitude will come through, so be positive. First impressions are lasting, so make yours a good one. You won't get a second chance.

Whoever represents the ministry by meeting or picking up a visitor should know about the ministry, city, and country and have a positive attitude about it. When arriving in a new country or city, visitors often bond with the first person they meet. In a new situation, guests will also feel more secure once they know a bit about the area and the people.

The first physical contact between host and guest is often at the airport or the door. Be on time for your guest's arrival. Offer a smile, identify yourself, and greet the person by name. Extend your hand for a firm handshake. Some children and young adults may be unfamiliar with shaking hands, but it is a welcome gesture among older people and Europeans of any age. Saying "hello" is always appropriate, but many may consider the greeting "hi" too casual.

Be aware of personal space. Generally, two to three feet between people is comfortable. The higher a person's rank or status, the more space should be given in deference. For instance, you could stand closer to an established friend than you would to the political leader of a foreign country.

Be careful about touching people you don't know. A touch on the elbow or shoulder might be okay. Touching heads or waists of strangers usually is not advisable. But hugs, embraces, or kisses might be a typical part of greeting. It all depends on the person and his or her cultural background. If in doubt, wait to see what the other person seems to find comfortable.

Language may be a barrier. It is a natural tendency to raise one's voice or shout when there is a language difference. Remember that your guest speaks a different language but can probably hear your normal tone of voice!

If you do understand the same language, put your guest at ease by making small talk, chatting about light topics. In many cultures, this is an essential prologue to true conversation. Offer some information about yourself and the ministry, and ask a few questions about things that might interest your visitor. Inquire about his or her home, job, family, or ministry. Don't be afraid to use appropriate humor; laughter creates a satisfying bond between people. Choose relevant topics and suitable words, expressions, and questions. Avoid getting too personal. A little homework done on your guest's home country and culture will go a long way as you begin to converse. Avoid making stops for personal errands on the way home.

Formal introduction guidelines are still suitable today. In general, introduce team members to guests and members of other organizations, lower ranking people to their superiors, and younger people to their elders.

When introducing a guest to others, use the visitor's title or role. This immediately makes him or her feel valued. Use the guest's full name, which gives dignity, unless you are asked to address the person less formally. In some cultures, only immediate family and close friends use first names and nicknames. Introduce individuals by their own titles or roles, not just as the husband or wife of someone. Speak clearly, slowly, and loudly so names will be understood. If you make a mistake in your introduction, make the correction and move on. In a group setting, people often introduce themselves and start conversations on their own.

Remembering names can be challenging, especially when a group of visitors arrives. Repeating a name several times makes it familiar. Use the guest's name frequently in conversation. Some people find word associations helpful for remembering names. Since our mission is international, so are the names of our guests. Pay special attention to the pronunciations.

INTRODUCING A SPEAKER

If hospitality involves introducing a speaker, remember that this practice establishes a speaker's credibility and builds audience enthusiasm for both the speaker and topic. Give a brief two- to three-minute introduction, drawing attention to the speaker rather than yourself. Check beforehand to ensure that your remarks, your pronunciation of the speaker's name, and any titles used are accurate. Adapt your remarks and level of formality to the occasion or event. Avoid over-praising the speaker or setting unrealistic expectations of the message. Don't assume that everyone in the audience knows the speaker. Tailor your introduction to the topic and the interests of the audience. Dress to honor the speaker. Show honor and respect while creating a sense of anticipation in the audience. End your introduction with the speaker's name one last time.

SCRIPTURES ON COMMUNICATION

Let's consider these scriptures compiled by Darlene Cunningham.

But the wisdom from above is first pure, then peaceable, gentle, reasonable, then full of mercy and good fruits, unwavering, without hypocrisy.

James 3:17 NASB

Let no unwholesome word proceed from your mouth, but only such a word as is good for edification according to the need of the moment, so that it will give grace to those who hear.

Ephesians 4:29 NASB

Reprove a wise man and he will love you. Give instruction to a wise man and he will be still wiser. Teach a righteous man and he will increase his learning.

Proverbs 9:8–9 NASB

Set a guard, O LORD, over my mouth; keep watch over the door of my lips.

Psalm 141:3 NASB

"If anyone has ears to hear, let him hear. . . . Take care what you listen to. By your standard of measure it will be measured to you; and more will be given to you besides."

Mark 4:23–24 NASB

He is on the path of life who heeds instruction, but he who ignores reproof goes astray.

Proverbs 10:17 NASB

The good man out of the good treasure of his heart brings forth what is good; and the evil man . . . brings forth what is evil; for his mouth speaks from that which fills his heart.

Luke 6:45 NASB

He who conceals a transgression seeks love, but he who repeats a matter separates intimate friends.

Proverbs 17:9 NASB

Pleasant words are a honeycomb, sweet to the soul and healing to the bones.

Proverbs 16:24 NASB

Like apples of gold in settings of silver is a word spoken in right circumstances.

Proverbs 25:11 NASB

A gentle answer turns away wrath, but a harsh word stirs up anger.

Proverbs 15:1 NASB

A man has joy in an apt answer, and how delightful is a timely word!

Proverbs 15:23 NASB

Death and life are in the power of the tongue, and those who love it will eat its fruit.

Proverbs 18:21 NASB

But speaking the truth in love, we are to grow up in all aspects into Him who is the head, even Christ.

Ephesians 4:15 NASB

The lips of the wise spread knowledge, but the hearts of fools are not so.

Proverbs 15:7 NASB

A man will be satisfied with good by the fruit of his words.

Proverbs 12:14 NASB

Let your speech always be with grace, as though seasoned with salt, so that you will know how you should respond to each person.

Colossians 4:6 NASB

Let the words of my mouth and the meditation of my heart be acceptable in your sight, O LORD, my rock and my Redeemer.

Psalm 19:14 NASB

getting ready: planning, preparing, and receiving

THAT YOU RECEIVE HER IN THE LORD IN A MANNER

WORTHY OF THE SAINTS, AND THAT YOU HELP HER IN

WHATEVER MATTER SHE MAY HAVE NEED OF YOU.

ROMANS 16:2 NASB

After you have invited a guest or accepted a request, more specific tasks will be necessary in preparation for the visitor's arrival. In any case, there will be work involved, but you have a choice to consider it a labor of love.

What is the purpose of hospitality? To provide rest and refreshment for those God brings our way. We want our guests to feel welcome and comfortable and to enjoy their time with us. Romans 15:32 expresses the desire of a guest: "That I may come to you with joy by the will of God and find refreshing rest in your company" (NASB).

While anxiety and panic may be common reactions, it is possible to feel calm and peaceful as you ready a place for visitors. Pray and prepare your heart before your guest arrives. Time spent in prayer and reading encouraging scriptures will add energy to your steps.

Praying and preparing for expected guests has always been important to me. When I lived in Lausanne, my mother and sister were planning to visit. Not only was it my sister's first cross-cultural experience, it was also my mom's birthday. I wanted to make it a special time for both of them. My family and I wanted to show them specific things in the area, including my son Nathan's favorite castle. I had to prayerfully prepare in my heart for this visit, taking into account their jet lag, our planned activities, and how to truly honor and welcome them. It was such fun to prepare their welcome baskets, including our family's new favorite treats and personal mementos from Switzerland. A visit is much more special when the host puts personal thought, prayer, and care into planning and preparation.

Questions to ask as your family or ministry team prepares to receive guests:

- Are we cheerful givers?
- What will we offer?
- Will we give our best?
- Will we be generous?
- Is our welcome warm?

WHO ARE SOME OF OUR GUESTS?

YWAM ministries serve as home bases for staff members and temporary homes for students attending classes—all under the oversight of the hospitality department. The hospitality ministry provides a place where staff and students can welcome friends and relatives who visit them.

We also have the privilege of welcoming many men and women of God as guest speakers in our schools. Other guests include staff members from other ministry bases, friends and relatives of staff and students, and visitors inquiring about our ministry in general or a particular area of interest. Political dignitaries and community leaders may also visit or observe our ministry. Some guests come for a few hours and some for a few days. Some need only a refreshing beverage, some come for a meal, and others need overnight accommodations. Many of our guests are Christians, but some are not. No matter who they are, each person who comes is important, and we are eager to serve those that God brings our way.

GUIDELINES FOR GETTING READY

A few practical principles are necessary to get ready for ministry guests. Set up guidelines according to your family's or individual ministry's accommodations, schedules, and staff availability. Consider the following:

- How many guest rooms do you have?
- What is the guest housing request process?
- Will staff be allowed to have personal guests stay in their rooms?
- Are there families in the neighborhood or surrounding community who would open a guest room to visitors if needed?
- Will guests be asked to participate in the community?

- Are guest visits restricted at any time (for example, during the first week of class, holiday periods, or staff conferences)?
- Are there special dates for "open house" when many guests would be welcome?
- How much turnover time is needed between guests to clean rooms, wash laundry, and other tasks?
- Will visitors who are able to contribute be charged for meals or asked to donate?
- Will vacationing guests be accepted?
- Are there any legal considerations for nonlocal visitors? For example, some international ministries require registration of all guests with the local authorities.

Know how many guests you can comfortably accommodate at any one time, and limit visitors accordingly. This may vary as circumstances dictate. For example, you may choose not to accept visitors during a busy time for the ministry. Or you may take in extra guests when teams are away on outreach.

Have guidelines in place for handling specific situations such as extended visits or guests with special ministry needs. The ministry leader may be consulted as to the suitability of each situation. Some guests, especially locals, will be flexible about when they come and how long they stay. Others have fixed schedules or are passing through and may take priority for certain dates.

Potential guests should register through one person before their stay. This prevents double booking of guest rooms and allows for planning of meals and supplies. It also facilitates recording of guest needs and requested activities or personal ministry. Staff members should register their own personal guests. It is important that the ministry leadership knows who is visiting at all times.

Before a guest's arrival, inform the ministry receptionist and leader as well as other leaders affected by the visit. In addition, notify the kitchen staff of the number of guests and any special dietary needs so they can prepare enough for mealtimes.

Assemble a hospitality file folder with information about each guest, correspondence notes, purpose of visit, specific health or accommodation needs, and other details.

As the guest's arrival date draws near, confirm the expected date, time, and means of arrival. Be sure to cover any last-minute details, such as transportation needs or other requests. Designate a meeting place, especially at an airport or train station, so you can find each other in the crowd.

Anticipate your guest's needs before arrival. Imagine what you would need if you came for a visit. Be ready to provide three basics: housing, meals, and transportation. International guests usually need extra attention for jet lag, currency exchange, and cultural adjustment. Consider your ministry's schedule and decide how to best serve him or her within your time parameters. Refresh your memory: does this person have special dietary needs? What is the guest's schedule like?

Consider personalities, backgrounds, professions, cultures, and experiences when visitors who don't know each other must share a guest room. Be careful about who rooms together. It's our privilege and our responsibility to prayerfully consider how guests will respond to one another.

Prepare and freshen the guest room, then check it one more time. Put fresh flowers, a welcome basket, and a card or small gift in the room. Check the toiletry basket and supply of towels. Does the room look and smell fresh?

When possible, allow your guest the luxury of sleeping in. This break in a busy person's routine may be a time for a little extra R&R.

Day guests will be pleased to have a room available for peace and quiet while they refresh themselves and prepare for ministry or speaking. Provide a beverage and snack or a meal. Link each day guest with a host person for thirty minutes to an hour to show the visitor around and introduce him or her to others. Be prepared to share and answer questions about your ministry and the surrounding community or country. Offer to take the visitor on a tour. If you have more than one day guest, try to group them together for information and tours. This will save you from repeating yourself and allow the guests to become acquainted with one another.

HOSTING SPECIFIC GUESTS

Parents of staff and students

Take good care of parents! Many of them have given up close contact with their children who have joined your ministry. Some parents may be concerned that their children have become involved in a radical group. They may need evidence of the soundness of your ministry and reassurance that they are welcome to visit. Some young adults are away from home for the first time, and their parents may just need to know that their children are comfortable and safe.

The father of one staff member was not supportive of his son's involvement with YWAM. When this dad came to visit, he was surprised to see the friendliness toward him and the love in our community. In particular, the hospitality staff blessed him. This man began to speak favorably about the ministry, and his church started sending regular support checks to his son. Give parents some extra TLC. If available, your nicest guest room is a special place for them to stay.

Visiting staff from other ministries

Don't overlook these special guests. Some come to you in need of rest, and others come to observe or share your ministry.

Unexpected guests

Expect the unexpected. You are bound to have visitors arrive on your doorstep with no prior notice. Perhaps they are passing through and need a place to stay. Or maybe they had planned to come but forgot to let you know. Though it may appear to be an interruption to you, it could be a divine appointment from God.

When an unexpected guest arrives, extend a warm welcome. Offer a seat and a refreshing drink. Then excuse yourself, take a deep breath, and think about possibilities for meeting your guest's needs. If space allows, it is wonderful to have a spare guest room always ready. If you don't have a central place for hospitality, ask staff members if they would be willing to take in guests from time to time.

MEETING AND RECEIVING GUESTS

A homecoming can take place in a bus terminal, at a train station, or on a sidewalk. While waiting, we may experience anticipation, hope, and longing. Then the face of the expected one appears, and we look into that person's eyes and express our welcome into the home of our hearts.

A host should be designated to greet each guest on arrival. If transportation to your ministry is needed, make arrangements for someone to meet the visitor at the airport, train station, or other location. A hospitality team member can meet most guests, but it is nice to have ministry leaders pick up speakers and other leaders. School staff can arrange to pick up school speakers.

Know the cultural practices of your guest's home country. Some men would be offended to be picked up by a woman. People of important stature may expect to be met by a ministry leader rather than a hospitality host.

Clean your vehicle, making room for passengers and luggage, and check the gas gauge. Dress neatly and appropriately. Call ahead to confirm arrival times. If needed, create a sign, and plan to stand in a visible location. Don't take small children with you if possible. Many travelers arrive tired and too weary to deal with active little ones.

For the comfort and security of your guest, be prompt. A waiting host gives people a sense of being wanted. It is a lonely feeling to arrive in a strange place and have no one there to meet you. For security reasons, it is especially important to be on time when picking up young women or guests who arrive late in the evening.

You might also observe a traditional way of welcoming visitors in your ministry's culture. In Europe, a bouquet of flowers from the market is appropriate. In Hawaii, a fresh flower lei is a traditional greeting, and I have even made them quickly on the way to the airport to greet guests. These welcome gestures are wonderful blessings to guests.

To help visitors feel welcome, try meeting needs before they are expressed. On the way from the airport or train station, begin to orient the guest to your daily schedule, special events, and other activities. Let them know about meals, laundry, and speaking schedules. Always try to be one step ahead. People often do not like to ask questions or make special requests, feeling it must be a bother to us. Let them know that it is your privilege to meet their needs.

Inform the visitor of the suggested dress code of your ministry. Point out the nearest shower and toilet (and how to flush it, if needed) and any idiosyncrasies of the home, such as electricity or plumbing challenges, purity of tap water, or noisy pipes. What is normal to us may not be normal to visiting guests, especially those from different nations.

The first time I arrived in Holland after a long flight and car ride, I needed to use the bathroom (*toilet* in Dutch). For the life of me, I couldn't figure out how to flush the toilet! I tried everything. Embarrassed, I asked my hostess how to do it. She graciously told me, "You pull on the pipe!"

Tell the guest how to contact the hospitality team with questions, concerns, or requests. A detailed hospitality notebook, left permanently in each guest room, will be a valuable help for visitors in need of information after you leave.

Suggest a tour of the ministry, either on arrival or after the guest has rested awhile. Your guest might like a full tour of the ministry or an abbreviated tour of the main buildings. Or perhaps the visitor has a specific area of interest and would most like to see certain projects or departments.

A hospitality staff member or another ministry representative may lead a tour. Present the tour in the visitor's first language if possible. Recruit a bilingual staff member to lead or translate as needed. The tour should include an explanation of ministries as well as the physical layout of the facilities. Remember that people, not buildings, are what makes your ministry what it is! As you visit each department, chat with a staff member if one is available.

Emphasize the unique or positive aspects of your ministry, and tell what God has been doing there. Be ready to answer questions about your ministry, its history, or your base in particular (be versed in these areas beforehand). Helpful aids include a photo album of activities, a slide show, a written history of the ministry, and videos.

Introduce the visitor to staff and students you encounter. Direct the guest to the appropriate people for specific information, personal ministry, and other related activities. Set up an appointment with the leader or other coworkers if appropriate. Make sure your guest knows how and where to exchange currency, make phone calls, buy stamps, send or receive mail, and use a copier or Internet connection.

Accompany the guest to the dining room for meals and to meeting rooms for gatherings. Have a staff member sit with new visitors until they are acquainted with others. Coffee time or a meal may be a good time to socialize.

Ask how you can help with laundry, errands, or childcare. Find out what the guest would like to do or see while in the area. If he or she has been with you longer than a week, offer to clean the room, change the sheets, and provide fresh towels. Check periodically during the stay to answer any questions or accommodate unmet needs.

DEPARTURES

When guests depart, you will again need to arrange any transportation or other practical needs. Someone should be available to see them off, including a ride to the airline boarding gate or train entry if necessary.

The day before guests leave, ask if there is any laundry to be done. And check for clean laundry that they may have left in the laundry room.

Anticipate guests' needs in the next several hours and try to meet them. For example, a beverage and snacks for the journey ahead may be appropriate. Again, we may give special attention to speakers or other leaders as they leave us. The next recipients of their ministry will appreciate the time and trouble we have saved them.

what to do when a guest arrives

☐ Make sure a host is present.

☐ Greet the guest and offer a drink and snack.

☐ Give the guest a schedule of meal times and location.

☐ Offer to give a tour (remembering that it is about the service and people, not the office!).

☐ Know the history and vision of the ministry.

☐ Show the guest how to buy stamps, make phone calls, and connect to the Internet.

☐ Introduce the guest at meals or ask others to host them at meals.

☐ Arrange for the guest to be invited to other coworkers' rooms or homes.

☐ Communicate (in writing and verbally) with everyone who might have contact with the guest.

☐ Be sure to let these people know who is coming: receptionist, director, and representative from any ministry that could benefit from this guest.

☐ Keep some information on each guest in case you need it for reference.

☐ Find out the purpose of the visit.

☐ If required in your country, register the guest at the reception desk.

☐ Arrange for accompaniment if guests are not to wander through the ministry on their own. This is a security measure in some places.

☐ If guests would like to attend a lecture, check first with the school leader.

preparation for overnight guests checklist

☐ Guest name

_____

☐ Arrival date/time

_____

☐ Departure date/time

_____

☐ Arrival transportation arranged

☐ Accommodation prepared

☐ Meals arranged

☐ Ministry arranged

☐ Tours and sightseeing throughout visit arranged

☐ Appropriate welcome basket, toiletry basket, flowers, towels

☐ Change of linen if duration of stay is longer than one week

☐ Special needs: laundry, errands, babysitting, e-mail, phone calls, Internet

☐ Transportation during stay arranged

☐ Departure transportation arranged

transportation checklist

☐ Schedule vehicle use.

☐ Make sure vehicle runs properly, is clean, and is filled with gas.

☐ Call airport or station beforehand to verify arrival time.

☐ If it's not you, carefully choose the person to pick up guest.

☐ Ask a responsible leader to pick up speakers and leaders.

☐ Don't have men pick up women or women pick up men, if inappropriate in your guest's culture or yours.

☐ Give some personal information about the guest to person who is picking him or her up.

☐ Don't take small children when it isn't appropriate.

☐ Dress neatly; you are the guest's first impression of the ministry you represent.

☐ Be on time, especially for young women or late evening arrivals.

☐ Have a neatly written sign, and stand in a place where you can be seen.

☐ Greet guest warmly.

☐ Begin orientation with some positive aspects about your ministry.

☐ Do not run errands or go shopping on your way back to the ministry location.

the guest room: attitudes, actions, and finishing touches

I KNOW THAT THIS MAN WHO OFTEN COMES OUR WAY IS A
HOLY MAN OF GOD. LET'S MAKE A SMALL ROOM ON THE ROOF
AND PUT IN IT A BED AND A TABLE, A CHAIR AND A LAMP FOR
HIM. THEN HE CAN STAY THERE WHENEVER HE COMES TO US.

2 KINGS 4:9–10

One guest room after another to clean and prepare can be an endless job within a hospitality ministry. We may be tempted to cry, "Oh no, not another one!" But from another perspective, hospitality is an opportunity to serve others and make a difference in their lives and even in the world. In fact, hospitality is a biblical mandate. In 1 Peter 4:9–10 we are encouraged to "offer hospitality to one another without grumbling. Each one should use whatever gift you have received to serve others, as faithful stewards of God's grace in its various forms."

Our desire regarding those who arrive at our ministry or home, whether staying for a time or just passing through, is for us to receive the maximum that they have to offer us, and to give our maximum in order to minister to their needs. It is easy to let guests slip in and out without really making contact with them or learning God's purpose for their visits. We need to fully extend ourselves.

The disciples at Emmaus followed the custom of their time when they said to their unknown traveling companion, "Stay with us, for it is nearly evening; the day is almost over" (Luke 24:29). However, even today we can take a cue from them and make our ministry a place of rest for weary travelers. We never know who might be in our midst. Provide a resting place—a place where guests can be quiet for a while to sort things out.

This woman quoted in 2 Kings 4:9–10 truly had a heart for hospitality. She saw a way that she could minister to one of the saints. As she saw to the details, such as a chair and a lamp, little did she know what a blessing this guest would be to her family! Who knows what guests God might send our way, and what effect we might have on each one.

On one occasion, a student's mother, who did not know the Lord, came to our ministry for a visit. The student was a bit nervous, so she asked our hospitality department to pray as we prepared a room for her mom. We prayed for God's angels to be present in that particular guest room. During the visit, the angels did indeed make their presence known, and the mother accepted Jesus as her personal savior in the quietness of that guest room.

Often we take surroundings for granted, yet they have a great effect on people. As we prepare a haven for each guest, we prepare a place for God to work. God is a God of beauty as well as order, and he has given us beautiful things to enjoy. One manifestation of his image in us is our ability to arrange things and create pleasing, comfortable surroundings.

No matter what your resources are, you can outfit your guest room in a manner worthy of the saints. Do what you can to create a cheerful, beautiful room. Pray for inspiration as you decorate, for the peace of each anticipated guest as you prepare for his or her arrival, and even for joy as you clean the room following a guest's departure.

Gracious hosting requires consideration, planning, preparation, and serving. We are to anticipate and meet the basic needs of our guests. Then we can feel free to add individual touches that make the room more attractive and functional.

A warm and refreshing atmosphere might vary from ministry to ministry and from area to area. I have decorated guest rooms in several countries, using very different furnishings and decorative items. Each time the results have been comfortable and beautiful. In Uganda we hung African batiks on the walls. Dutch lace and lots of plants created a cozy feeling in Holland. Montana guest rooms were furnished with wildlife motif lamps and log-framed beds. Batik fabrics were used for curtains and bedding in Indonesia.

COLOR

Color is a magic ingredient that can make a room come alive, make it sing, and give those who enter a happy, cheerful feeling. Color can also make a room seem depressing or dull, bringing a moody feeling on its occupants.

Color sets the atmosphere in a room; it creates a mood and character that affects those who enter it. With boundless colors to choose from, there are countless ways to decorate. Keep in mind what you want a room to communicate to its occupants. Most likely you want them to feel rested and at peace rather than anxious and fidgety. Cool sea and forest colors such as blues, greens, and purples tend to promote rest and dreamy peacefulness, while warm sunshine colors like reds, yellows, and oranges evoke an atmosphere of work, busyness, and energy.

Imagine if the sky were orange and the grass red. The emotional impact would make us wild! God knew which miraculous array of colors would provide the best ambience for his children to live in—soft blue sky, green grass, rich brown earth, and golden sun.

Color can also trick the eye into thinking rooms are smaller, larger, lighter, more elegant, or more up to date than they actually are. Dark colors bring the walls in and close in a room. They are ideal for making a huge room seem less cavernous. Light colors open up a room and make it feel larger.

All the colors may be used in decorating as long as their impact is considered. Red tends to rev up the mood, but pink is gentler, and pale pink is very quiet. Deep rose is a versatile background color, especially pretty with cream and soft greens. The mellow glow of peach sets a warm, relaxing mood that's dreamy and romantic, but orange is likely to stimulate your appetite. Yellow is for intellectuals with imagination and lofty dreams. Green is a soothing color, giving the effect of a peaceful forest. Blue elicits a deep response of tranquility, satisfying the human need for a serene atmosphere. Brown is earthy; gray is cautious. Black is a sophisticated color, out of the ordinary, and should be used sparingly on walls, but it makes a great accent. In large quantities, purple is considered depressing and unbalanced. A little purple goes a long way, so it should be used more for accents.

Colors can be mixed in different combinations. A confetti of vivid colors will make a room burst with excitement. These shades are thrilling—they bloom with life and make us feel elated. A marble of soft colors can have a much more quieting effect, promoting reflection and contemplation in a room that is cozy, restful, and inviting. And then there are mixes of vivid shades with soft ones, which create interesting effects as well.

The careful use of color allows for many shades and hues in any size room. In small rooms, lighter walls with dark accents allow for a use of many color depths while visually enlarging the room. Similarly, a warm but cheery color like yellow may be used in accents without making the total effect a busy one. Soft, light-hearted colors may set the tone, while bolder, brighter colors are used sporadically for details. Choose a main color to use in approximately 80 percent of the room and a complementary color for the other 20 percent. Use other coordinating colors as accents.

In Uganda, we had two guest rooms that were cheery with beautiful African cloth. In Indonesia, fabrics bought at a market provided color and texture. In Switzerland, fluffy duvets were covered with colorful cloth.

Lighting plays a major role in hospitality. Even a porch light has a part, sending out a greeting to arriving guests. Lighting creates much of the atmosphere in a room. A welcoming guest room will have light coming from different levels, with overhead lighting or a tall lamp complemented by table lamps. In areas where the electricity can go out quickly, it's wise to have a flashlight or a candle and matches available in the room.

The thoughtful furnishing of a room can work wonders. Furniture should be adequate and suitable. The most important item in a guest room is a bed. Make sure it is a comfortable one! Outfit it with linens, blankets, and pillows that are in good condition. Other appropriate furniture may include a table or desk with chair, a bedside table, and a bookcase that offers appropriate reading material and shelves for other items. Try to keep your guest rooms neutral in gender. Avoid an overly feminine or masculine room; that way anyone will feel comfortable in it.

Each guest room should include:

- Good lighting source (overhead and reading lamps)
- Comfortable chair (a place to sit other than on the bed)
- Place to sit and write (desk or table and chair)
- Correct number of beds
- Children's beds / cribs if needed
- For each bed: mattress cover, pillow, blankets or duvet
- Extra blankets and pillows
- Coordinating curtains and bedspreads
- Towels and washcloths
- Adequate drawer and closet space, coat tree
- Plenty of clothes hangers
- Large mirror (full length is nice)
- Wastebasket with plastic liners
- Alarm clock (avoid clocks that tick or chime)
- Temperature control (heating in cooler climates, fans in warmer climates)
- Radio or small television for newscasts
- Special needs for climate: mosquito netting, fan, heater, hot water bottle, or extra blankets
- Iron and hair dryer in local voltage
- Extra light bulbs of appropriate wattage
- Alternate light source in case of power outage
- Adequate supplies of toilet tissue, facial tissue
- Small sewing kit

- Toiletry basket
- First aid kit
- Teapot, set of cups, and saucers
- Tray with tea and coffee-making equipment and supplies
- Nearby shower, toilet, and sink with plug
- Key to room
- Guest book for memories and reflections
- Interesting magazines and books
- Stationery and postcards
- Information packet
- Personal welcome basket prepared for each guest

  Nice additions to guest rooms:
- Bath mat and floor rugs
- Laundry basket
- Placemats and napkins
- Can and bottle openers
- Radio with CD player and worship albums
- Small refrigerator
- Books, toys for children of different ages
- Voltage adaptors for foreign guests

Toiletry basket

Sometimes travelers arrive before their luggage does. They may be expected to meet new people, their hair is tousled, and they need to be refreshed. As a courtesy, a basket with toiletries is a nice addition to any guest room and another practical way of serving our guests. Items to include:

- Toothpaste
- Toothbrush
- Razor
- Bar of soap
- Pack of tissues
- Shampoo
- Deodorant
- Nail file
- Insect repellent
- Sunblock or sunscreen lotion
- Bandages

All of the listed items should be in sample sizes. You may want to include other articles that would be useful in your location or culture.

FINISHING TOUCHES

Most of us do not have large decorating budgets. But you can do a lot with a little money. Look around you for decorating inspiration. Local markets are great sources for textiles and other decorative items. Many household items can do double duty with both practical and decorative uses. Baskets used for storage are also nice to look at. On bookshelves, mix books and magazines with decorative items. Curtains and fabric decorations can be made from bed sheets.

I found this old quote in a Victorian magazine: "In some expectation of your coming I had already begun filling the vases with flowers so that you might have an attractive place to rest after your long journey." Flowers and plants add life and love to a room. Colorful blossoms create a festive and fragrant ambience.

Buy flowers at a local market or grow them yourself. In some areas you are free to pluck wildflowers off of roadside bushes or out of neighboring fields. Flowers unique to your area are a special touch. Try a stem of orchids in Asia or a bunch of meadow flowers in Switzerland. Flowers need not be displayed in bouquets; a single blossom in a bud vase can be lovely. When fresh flowers are not available, dried or silk flowers will brighten a guest room. Houseplants also add a warm touch (remember to keep them watered).

Don't forget to acclimatize the room. In a hot climate, include a fan and mosquito netting if necessary. A space heater, extra blankets, and a hot water bottle are appropriate in cold climates. Spend a night in your guest room to see for yourself how comfortable it is and to determine what is missing or what might be a nice added touch.

A well-decorated and equipped guest room will serve you and your guests for many years to come. Once it has been pleasantly decorated and furnished, all it needs is regular cleaning and special touches.

BEFORE A GUEST'S ARRIVAL

Each time a guest is expected, prepare the room by cleaning it thoroughly. Make the bed with freshly laundered sheets, and put out fresh towels. Allow two sets of towels per person, and fold them neatly and creatively, with no tags showing. Put out a fresh bar of soap with each set of towels. Check the supplies in the toiletry basket and replenish as necessary. Add flowers and a welcome basket, and you are ready to receive your guest!

The toiletry basket will have different contents according to what is customarily used and available. Again, offer what is culturally appropriate in your area. In cold climates, flowers may not be available in winter. The main point is to provide fresh, clean, personal touches in the room.

If your ministry involves students and receives teams of people, you might consider special preparation of student rooms. In John 14:2 Jesus says to his disciples, "my Father's house has many rooms. . . . I am going there to prepare a place for you." Let us remember that just as Jesus was preparing a place for his followers, we are asked to prepare rooms for the students who come to our ministries.

Attention should be given to this preparation, as the room will be home for a time. Provide bedding for those who have traveled from afar; a pillow can fill an entire suitcase! First impressions are lasting, and this may be the student's initial introduction to the world of missions.

When preparing a guest room, think through and apply the five senses (vision, smell, taste, sound, touch). What visual effect will there be? Will colors be coordinated, and will the room look neat and tidy? Will the room smell fresh and clean? Is the room located in a quiet area or next to the busiest hub of the ministry? Will the sense of touch be pleased by various textures and fabrics? And finally, will there be something for the taste buds to enjoy—fresh fruit or a sweet treat? The most pleasant guest havens offer satisfaction for all five senses.

- Vision: looks neat and clean with coordinated colors
- Smell: a fresh scent greets those who enter
- Taste: fresh fruit, savory and sweet snacks available
- Sound: located in a quiet area of the base
- Touch: appropriate fabrics and textures included in décor

HOUSING TEAMS, SPEAKERS, AND OTHER GUESTS

In YWAM we believe in the "live/learn" concept. When students and staff live and work together, they learn from one another. Community housing has many benefits. It facilitates a spirit of giving, sharing, generosity, and cooperation. It allows for growth and experience in cross-cultural living. But it is not without its challenges, and some special considerations will help smooth the way.

Housing considerations for a single guest

When individual rooms are not available, single guests must share rooms. Here are some practical guidelines for assigning rooms.
- Treat everyone equally, avoiding favoritism. Actual or perceived inequality, whether accidental or intentional, can lead to problems.
- Our first priority is to find the best living situation for each person.

- Consider personalities when placing roommates. This requires prayerful and often quick assessments. A shy person can benefit greatly from an outgoing roommate.
- Avoid assigning those who work together to live as roommates. This will give each person a greater breadth of fellowship at a ministry location.
- Generally, it is easiest for people of similar ages to room together. However, this depends on individual personalities.
- Each housing unit should have one person with the strength and spiritual maturity to serve as house leader when necessary. This is especially important with young men.
- With very young students, a parental figure may be needed. A more mature person can be assigned to a room as a stable leader; assign another older person in the room for fellowship.
- Avoid assigning a short-term student to room with a long-term student or staff member. This eliminates multiple changes and adjustments.
- Generally, it is best to separate staff and students. Roommates are then more likely to share common hours, schedules, classes, interests, and mindsets.
- A larger house or apartment with a group of single men or single women requires a designated house coordinator who will administrate and organize household chores, rent payments, and purchases of shared groceries and household products.
- When living problems arise, allow time for issues to resolve. If serious challenges still remain, consult ministry leadership.
- Be flexible, knowing that mistakes will happen. Moves are possible if the necessity arises.
- All moves should be processed by a housing team.

Housing for families

In YWAM we are committed to the family as a team in ministry. Each family member is valued as a part of that team.

By marrying, a couple has become one entity, functioning as a pair in the community and as individual members of the group. Encourage them to have time alone together, which is best facilitated by giving them a room of their own.

It is clear that a husband and wife have a place in ministry. But let's not forget what a blessing children are to a community.

When planning housing, respect each family unit, and the families will respect the mission in return. No matter how tight our quarters, each family unit must remain intact. Decisions on housing should be made with the following considerations:

- length of commitment to the ministry
- type of commitment to the ministry
- ages and genders of children.

A family of five would need more space than a family of three. A teenage boy and his teenage sister should each have a private area, if not a separate room.

guest room setup

Hanging towels

2 bath towels
2 hand towels
2 face cloths
1 bath mat (hung over tub edge)

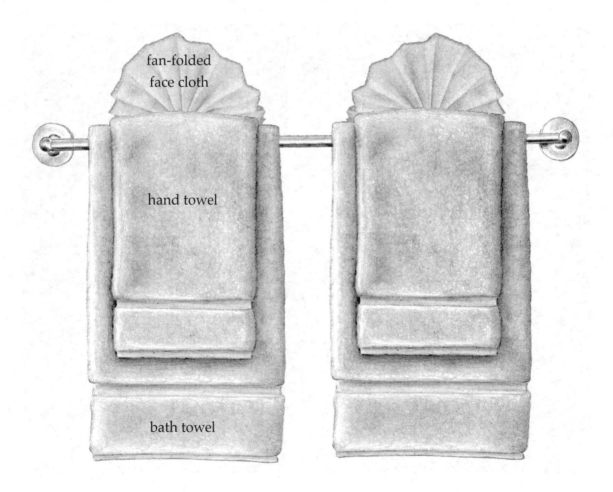

fan-folded
face cloth

hand towel

bath towel

guest room setup

Folded towels

Suggestions for laying towels on the bed:

Stacked towel set

A small bar of soap is always a nice addition.

Fold a bath towel in thirds. Stack a folded face cloth on top. Place a bar of soap on the very top.

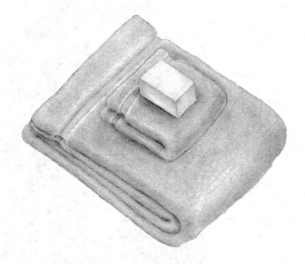

Rolled towel set

Roll up a towel, fold a face cloth and drape it over the towel.

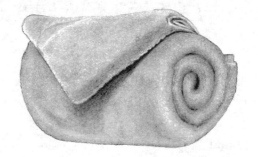

Fan-shaped towel set

Fold a bath towel in half. Wrap a face cloth around the middle. Tuck a bar of soap inside.

guest room setup

Basket

coffee, decaf, tea, creamer, sugar, sugar substitute, and stirrers

Dishes

hot pot	sharp knife
1 plate	2 mugs
1 knife	1 fork
can opener	basket
2 glasses	turn mugs and glasses upside down
1 spoon	refill basket daily
3–4 napkins	use matching mugs, glasses, cutlery

basic room preparation checklist

☐ Adequate and suitable furniture

☐ Correct number of beds

☐ Children's beds if needed

☐ Appropriate window coverings

☐ Mattress cover sheet

☐ Bedding and pillow, especially for those traveling from afar

☐ Clothes hangers

☐ Waste baskets

guest room pre-arrival checklist

☐ Name sign on door

☐ Personalized welcome card

☐ Welcome basket

☐ Welcome information book

☐ Beverages available

☐ Bed freshly made

☐ Fresh towels, folded on bed or displayed in guest bathroom

☐ Toiletry basket

☐ Extra roll of toilet paper

☐ Clean, fresh scent

☐ Comfortable room temperature

☐ Lamp turned on for evening arrival

guest room daily checklist

Without exception, a hospitality team member must check each morning with the guest, asking to help with laundry, errands, phone calls, and mail. Find out the best time for this communication to take place during the guest's stay.

☐ Dust all surfaces

☐ Clean window ledges, dressers, chairs, inside cupboards

☐ Straighten reading materials

☐ Check supplies in room

☐ Replace towels

☐ Empty garbage, wash container if necessary

☐ Check closets and drawers for anything guests might have left

☐ Wash coffee maker if necessary

☐ Polish mirrors

☐ Check light bulbs and replace burned-out ones

☐ Make beds and replace soiled linens if needed

☐ Vacuum if necessary

☐ Clean windows when needed

☐ Care for plants or, for fresh flowers, freshen up the water and bouquet

☐ Take dirty laundry to laundry room

☐ Wash dishes and return where they belong

☐ Replenish guest information packet with necessary information

guest room daily checklist (cont.)

If you have included options to make beverages, make sure the preparation area is clean and tidy. Replenish anything that has been used up. I usually put all of the beverage items on a tray. It is easy to transfer and also handy for guests to move around if they need more space. Use quantities that are appropriate for the guests' stay. Keep the tray clean and replace any soiled napkins.

☐ Coffee

☐ Creamer

☐ Tea bags

☐ Coffee filters

☐ Glasses

☐ Napkins

Bathroom:

☐ Clean toilet

☐ Wipe out sink and bathtub and replace old bars of soap

☐ Mop floor

☐ Shake out rug, wash weekly

☐ Replace toilet paper

a warm welcome

SO THAT I MAY COME TO YOU IN JOY BY THE WILL OF GOD

AND FIND REFRESHING REST IN YOUR COMPANY.

ROMANS 15:32 NASB

What a special feeling it is to be welcomed, to walk into an unfamiliar place and find a warm greeting and people willing to help with every aspect of your stay. You know immediately that you have been expected, that someone has prepared for your arrival.

Why is it so important to say, "Welcome"? Because it communicates our delight in a guest's arrival and helps with the initial bonding experience between guest and host. Welcoming guests is a wonderful act of generosity and an accurate reflection of the values of our mission: we care about people.

When guests arrive and put their bags down, one of the first rooms they visit is the guest room. As a host, fill it with personal touches that say, "You are welcome in this place." These touches may include a name card on the door, a welcome basket with a personal note, and an informational welcome packet.

NAME CARD

Have you ever been disoriented in unfamiliar surroundings and had difficulty finding your room? Perhaps you have even entered the wrong room by mistake. It's embarrassing, isn't it? This is why it is a nice gesture to hang an attractive card with the guest's name on each door. The card should be clearly and neatly written and may visually coordinate with the welcome card and basket that await your guest inside the room. A whiteboard on each door may also be used to write the name of each guest.

THE WELCOME BASKET

The hospitality welcome basket has become an important part of YWAM culture. It is evidence that we have anticipated the arrival of our guests and are eager to make them comfortable.

The complexity of each basket will vary depending on the number you must prepare, your budget, and the resources available to you. You might prepare baskets differently for men, women, and children. You may form an assembly line to fill small baskets for a group of students or conference attendees, but carefully personalize the contents of a welcome basket for each special guest. The container size may also vary; remember that a small mug full to the brim is much more effective than a large basket sparsely filled. The important thing is that your welcome is sincere and warm.

Perhaps you will use a cultural or national style for your ministry's welcome. Also, it is helpful to choose a specific theme for each conference or school when you have large numbers of baskets to prepare. When assembling baskets, consider colors, textures, flavors, and details. Be creative with repeat visitors, offering new surprises while remembering their favorites from previous visits.

My favorite act of service in hospitality is preparing to welcome a guest, especially if I have served that visitor before. I like to honor a guest by meeting a heartfelt need or desire. Bringing out favorite treats makes expectations rise, as every room becomes a celebration of bonds that will last a lifetime. It's fun to personalize welcomes! I try to make notes of people's favorites. Whenever YWAM speaker Maureen comes to visit, for example, she finds a Diet Coke in her welcome basket.

The container

The welcome basket container can be something other than an actual basket; use your imagination and look around you for inspiration. You might use a decorated paper bag or box. The container used for a welcome basket may be a gift in itself. A coffee mug can serve a dual purpose as a welcome container and a cup for coffee breaks. Jars or fabric bags will work as well.

The local culture may provide ideas for containers. Many African, Asian, and Pacific Island countries are known for specific types of baskets. Or consider an English teacup or tea towel, a wooden shoe for a Dutch *Welkom,* or a Texas bandanna lining a cowboy hat. When shopping in local markets or learning cultural handcrafts, keep welcome baskets in mind—you may be surprised at the imaginative containers you can come up with. You might use a "signature" container for all of your welcomes or vary them from guest to guest. Containers can be lined with cloth, paper napkins, tissue paper, or confetti; keep the room décor in mind to avoid clashing colors. The specific event you are hosting may offer an idea, and seasons or holidays may also inspire your welcome basket creativity. Preparing a welcome basket should never be a burden. Start simply, let your imagination flow, and have fun.

The contents

A welcome basket should include a greeting, food items, and a beverage. You might want to include a small gift from your locale. Make your basket attractive and colorful, including items that are pleasing to the eye and inviting to eat.

It is helpful to keep extra items on hand, such as small soaps, postcards, maps, and brochures of tourist attractions. Consider the culture and the theme of a school or conference for other ideas. A YWAM school of dance once included sweat towels and water bottles in its welcome baskets. One of our health care schools included small first aid kits. Also include small gifts for a speaker's spouse and children—guests enjoy bringing these home when they return from their travels.

Snacks and treats

Try to include fruit, a salty or savory snack, and a sweet treat in each basket. Home-made cookies or candy are a special touch. These provisions do not substitute for meals, but serve merely as snacks for those settling in before they want to leave the room or before they are comfortable to ask for food or drink. A source of protein such as cheese or nuts, fresh fruit, and water or another beverage can really hit the spot. Your thoughtfulness says, "You are important to us. We remembered!"

Some of these treats should represent the local culture whenever possible. In Switzerland a bar of Swiss chocolate is a part of welcome baskets; in Hawaii tropical fruits and macadamia nuts are unique; in Holland, Dutch chocolate, *stroopwafels* (waffle cookies), and other delicacies are specialties; African bases include ground nuts and dried fruit. Take-home items, such as a jar of Montana huckleberry jam, are also welcome.

Awaiting each member of our outreach team in the Ukraine was a special card and a delicious chocolate bar, nicely arranged in our rooms. It was a mass gift that appealed to everyone, and our team got hooked on chocolate for the remainder of our time there!

The greeting

A note of welcome may be written on a homemade or purchased greeting card, a picture postcard, or notepaper. You might create a card using local materials, such as batik in Indonesia or banana bark in Uganda. Use the native word or expression for "welcome," whatever that might be. A Swiss *Bienvenue* might be written on a card depicting cowbells or mountains, and a Hawaiian *Aloha* might feature brightly colored flowers. Small paintings, drawings, pieces of stitchery, or picture postcards featuring local scenery can become treasured keepsakes.

The greeting should express a general but warm welcome, including the guest's name. Use titles, if appropriate, and double-check the spelling of names. Add an encouraging scripture, writing it out in full, and include the reference. For guests who are not Christians, choose a generally understood scripture, or a quotation or short poem, which often ministers nicely. End your greeting with the name and phone number or the base location of a contact person.

A welcome card should express the following thoughts:

- Welcome to our ministry.
- We're glad you're here.
- We want this stay to be special for you.
- We are honored by your presence.

John and Julie Doe,
We are so glad that you are part of this community at this time. May God richly bless you during your stay here. It's a pleasure having you.
Mary Smith and the Hospitality Team
Phone 123-456-7890

Place the welcome card in a visible place in the basket. When more than one basket is placed in a room, identify each one with names on welcome card envelopes or tags. Baskets may be left open or fastened closed. A bit of ribbon, raffia, or even dried grass is a nice touch for a decorative bow or a functional closing.

THE WELCOME PACKET

When most people find themselves in unfamiliar situations, they want to know what's going on, what's expected of them, and where a particular room or location might be. One way of welcoming guests is to make sure they know those things. Verbal communication of schedules and details suffices only until it is forgotten or until facts are confused. This is a common challenge when guests arrive tired from traveling; often there is too much information to digest at once. Provide reference information in written form, to which guests can refer as often as necessary. A standard information packet that remains in the guest room will work for most situations, and inserts can be added for specific occasions or guests.

Information to include in your packet:

- Welcome letter signed by the ministry leader (in addition to a personal welcome card)
- Ministry information letter
- Map of base (may include surrounding areas)
- Meal schedule and dining room/snack bar locations
- Daily and weekly ministry schedules
- Phone directory
- Worship times, chapel availability
- Visitor/welcome center information
- Fire evacuation plan
- Policies/guidelines (quiet hours, parking, and phone use)
- On-site services available to guests, including locations, costs, and hours (these include bookstore, care closet, ice machine, laundry room, first aid supplies, library, resource center, mail room, telephone, Internet, vending machine, on-site store, safe deposit, fax machine, copy machine, recreation facilities, and childcare)
- Off-site services (these include hospital, doctors, dentists, check cashing, recreation, entertainment, grocery stores, drug stores, department stores, convenience stores, souvenir shops, restaurants, coffee shops, and hairdressers)
- Tourist information (local attractions, brochures, phone numbers)
- Recreation facilities
- Transportation schedules (local bus, train routes)
- Language phrases sheet

- Translation services
- Souvenir suggestions
- Safety precautions peculiar to area (e.g., sun, insects, drinking water)
- Hospitality team contact info

SPECIAL CONSIDERATIONS FOR NEW STUDENTS

Students arriving to attend schools should be welcomed in the same manner as all guests. However, because of the duration of their stay and special needs, we suggest a few extra preparations.

Place name signs on the door of each student and staff room. A welcome basket should be made for each student or couple. These should be identified with nametags or names on the welcome cards. This communicates that each student is expected and valued and is now a part of the community.

A welcome packet of information should be prepared for each student. This will serve as a guidebook regarding your base and the surrounding area. In addition to the welcome packet information prepared for other guests, the student packet may include more details for life at the base and in the community and country. Cultural information, holidays, language samplers, and general how-tos are all useful for students.

Name tags may be helpful for the first few days as class members and staff get acquainted. Assign a host staff member to each student who will pray before the student's arrival, greet him or her, and show the student around the building or base.

Additionally, a student roster (preferably with photos) should be prepared for administrative use at the ministry location. It should include a housing list and birthday and anniversary dates.

DEVELOPING A MINISTRY WELCOME CENTER

A welcome center will be the first impression of your ministry to visitors. Entryways should be warm and welcoming, putting our guests at ease. People are what ministry is all about; we don't ever want our guests to feel awkward or unwelcome.

As guests approach your main entry, they should see a pleasing sight. Step back and take a good look at the approach to your main entrance. What first impression does it give? How could it be improved to be more warm and welcoming? Consider the use of plants, flowers, a welcome mat, or a welcome sign. Make your place look and feel both well-run and welcoming.

Once your guests have entered your building, they will go to the reception area. Reception implies an act of receiving. Is your reception area ready to receive guests? Ministries vary in size and therefore in the space for reception. Basic requirements include a place to sit and a refreshing beverage to serve.

During a base renovation in Lausanne, Switzerland, we used a temporary reception area. A few feet beyond this area there was a bright sunroom, lovingly decorated in Swiss style with comfortable chairs and a beautiful view of the Alps. It was a peaceful place for guests to rest before going to their rooms or while waiting for their next course of action. We knew God had given us a broad scope of ministry as we greeted those whom God sent to us.

A range of guests might include:

- New staff members for initial welcome and orientation
- Visiting teachers who teach our courses
- New students who want to see the broader picture of God's call on their lives
- YWAM Mission Builders (providing ministry and facility development services to Christian ministries around the world)
- Politicians or heads of state
- Leaders of other mission groups or Christian organizations
- Local community, including service clubs, government agencies, vendors, pastors, church groups, educators, schools, tourists, the poor and needy, the unsaved, and skeptics

Generosity is a powerful hospitality investment. Some of our ministry locations give calendars, devotional magazines, pens, free lunches, snacks, childcare during tours, fresh-picked flowers, toys, gospel tracts, and Bibles. We've also provided wheelchair assistance and driving tours for those unable to walk.

Willing to go the "second mile" in serving is of great importance. In various situations and locations we have provided transport to and from hotels and airports. We've given tourist information. We've helped people find babysitters and informed them of our campus or church functions. We've recommended local churches. We've provided a donation bowl and given our guests the opportunity to give to missions, individuals, and mission projects. We've set up housing, interviews, conferences, luncheons, and put people together with other people. At times our hospitality has been extended to a week or a couple of days as we oversee the needs of certain ones who come back several times during their stay. We've also made arrangements for guests to sit in at various schools and given them applications and academic input.

VISITOR CENTER: STORIES FROM GUESTS

One parent shared the following observation: "We thought perhaps our daughter had gotten herself into a cult situation, but one of the things that has convinced us otherwise is the openness and hospitality shown to us at YWAM Kona and YWAM Amsterdam."

A middle-aged couple came to take a tour and check out Crossroads (Disciple-ship Training Schools designed for people age twenty-five and older). They said two of their kids had gone to two different DTSs, and the changes in their lives had so totally revolutionized the entire family that they wanted to get a dose as well.

A couple came and sat in on several classes, attended a prayer meeting, went to our luau, had an interview, and attended an evening service and social gathering on campus. They said, "We're so thankful that God gave us a Christian vacation!"

From a man in his fifties: "Many years ago, I felt God had called me to serve him in missions. I was young and had other plans, and like Jonah, I ran the other way. Now I'm sitting here and you are telling me that I have another chance and that I can still go and be used by God." He began to weep, and we had a time of prayer with him before he left with his application in hand.

An eighty-year-old local resident accepted Christ in the Visitor Center garden. He cried and thanked God for us being there to help him. The night before, he had prayed and asked God to please accept him.

A skeptical father whose daughter was attending a DTS came on a surprise visit, hoping to expose our "cult group." He didn't reveal his identity on the tour. The guides could sense his skepticism and prayed, and before he left, he paid his daughter's full tuition and the outreach fees of her roommate.

Some visitors said, "For years our son and daughter-in-law have been part of this organization, but even though they tried to tell us what it was all about, we couldn't quite accept what they were doing here. Thank you for making it so clear and understandable." They later sent in a donation to YWAM.

The importance of a warm welcome cannot be understated. One couple stopped by one of our YWAM ministry locations out of curiosity. They asked for a tour and were welcomed and led by the ministry leader. They were told how the ministry trained and sent out workers to the nations. The couple was so impressed that they now provide financial scholarships for international students in our training courses. The simple act of hospitality—taking time out of a busy schedule to show strangers a ministry—resulted in a lifelong partnership of sending missionaries to the nations.

This welcome letter example gives guests a name to refer to when they have questions or need information. Use it as a template.

Dear Guest,

Welcome to (name of location). We are delighted to have you here and desire to make your stay as enjoyable as possible. The information in this packet will help you become familiar with our operations. Please feel free to let us know if there is any way we can serve you.

You may contact our staff (give appropriate information for your location, including a name and phone number for the guest to contact after hours).

Once again, we welcome you and pray that the Lord will refresh you while you are here.

In his service,

(Name)

welcome checklist

Welcome basket for every guest

☐ Fresh fruit

☐ Sweet snack (cookies, chocolate, or something special from your culture)

☐ After long trips: substantial snacks such as nuts, raisins, trail mix, beef jerky

☐ Savory snack (crackers, pretzels, nuts)

A ministry receives a variety of guests. The following suggestions will help honor each guest with various welcoming touches.

Speakers, friends, parents, pastors, and representatives from other missions

☐ Personalized welcome card

☐ Welcome basket

☐ Flowers if available

☐ Toiletries basket

☐ Information packet

☐ Schedule during stay

☐ Extra drinks and snacks

☐ Postcards and stamps

☐ Door name card

welcome checklist

Students and other guests

☐ Welcome card with scripture   ☐ Door name card

☐ Welcome basket   ☐ Postcard of base or surrounding area

☐ Welcome packet

Children

☐ Welcome card   ☐ Small game, toy, or souvenir

☐ Small welcome basket

Conference attendees

☐ Welcome card with scripture   ☐ Chocolate or specialty from culture

☐ Small gift

welcome packet checklist

☐ Letter of welcome

☐ Map of ministry with location of dining room, offices, classrooms, snack bar, and anything else that would be helpful to guest

☐ Transportation options and schedules for buses, trains, and bicycle rentals

☐ Meal schedule and location, with weekend schedule if different from weekdays

☐ Laundry facility location and procedures

☐ First aid location

☐ Post office procedures

☐ Telephone location and instructions for international calls

☐ Availability of e-mail and computer hookups

☐ Emergency contact number, including police and fire numbers with directions to base location

☐ Special facilities available: weight room, swimming pool, news room, snack bar, library, bookstore, boutique, vending machines, visitor center

☐ Parking location if the guest has a car

☐ Schedule of base meetings, worship services that guests are welcome to attend

☐ Banking procedures, banking hours, and best place to exchange foreign currency

☐ Local sightseeing opportunities, including brochures

☐ Cultural warnings: specific insects, sun intensity, and water quality

☐ Shopping availability: local stores and times, markets to explore, best places to buy certain items

☐ Social interaction: appropriate greeting (handshake? cheek kissing?)

welcome packet checklist

☐ Local ministry performances during guest's stay: cultural events, performances, art show, or anything that your local base is involved with

☐ Cultural orientation: cultural background of base locale

☐ Social practices: host gift, thank-you note or gift

☐ A few words and phrases from the local language with pronunciations, such as:
Hello
Goodbye
Yes
No
Please
Thank you
My name is
What is your name?
Numbers 1–20

chapter 9

serving speakers

THE GENEROUS MAN WILL BE PROSPEROUS,

AND HE WHO WATERS WILL HIMSELF BE WATERED.

PROVERBS 11:25 NASB

When the YWAM international advisory board—a group of non-YWAM businessmen—travels to meetings, they forego five-star hotels in favor of staying on the ministry location with staff and students. They love our hospitality because they know it comes from our hearts.

However, not everyone has had this impression. A YWAM speaker visiting from New Zealand shared about hospitality experiences he'd had at various ministry locations around the world. He spoke with hilarity, and most of the crowd laughed at the predicaments and situations he'd been in. But I didn't find it funny; in fact, I was embarrassed to hear that he had been treated without honor or respect.

We are exhorted in scripture to honor the presence of God's messengers. Philippians 2:29 admonishes us to "welcome him in the Lord with great joy, and honor people like him." First Timothy 5:17–18 says, "The elders who rule well are to be considered worthy of double honor, especially those who work hard at preaching and teaching" (NASB).

We should give great amounts of attention and service to those with the greatest levels of responsibility. This is not to show preference, but to help balance the loads and extend the effectiveness of those who must reach many people. By serving them, we ease the weight of their routine tasks so that they can focus on study, prayer, counseling, and time with people.

There are many ways we can honor those whom the Lord releases to teach us. It is up to the hospitality ministry to offer comfortable accommodations, meals and snacks, and services such as doing laundry and running errands. But be careful not to take advantage of your access to a leader or speaker by expecting counseling or other attention whenever you deliver a meal. You are there to serve, not to be served.

THE SPEAKER'S QUARTERS

Provide a place where a speaker (and his or her family) can find peace and quiet within the busy atmosphere of the ministry. The speaker's quarters should have adequate space and furnishings for sleeping, eating, and meeting with others for counseling or prayer. Try to anticipate the speaker's needs and provide for them, which will free up time for ministry.

One YWAM speaker shared about the fatigue, stress, and spiritual pressure involved in traveling as a speaker. He considers a little comfort in the speaker's room as necessary for adequate rest and relaxation. He clarifies that speakers don't expect great luxury. They don't hesitate to go to developing countries and stay in rooms without electricity or water—pioneer situations are well understood, and speakers are ready to make sacrifices. But on established bases with Western comforts, our speakers should not be housed in conditions inferior to our own rooms or homes.

Added touches go a long way in making a speaker more comfortable. A hot pot or coffee maker with cups, filters, coffee, creamer, and sugar allow the speaker to prepare a hot drink early in the morning or late in the evening. A CD player with CDs, books in the speaker's language, ministry books and brochures, and even a television are helpful additions to the room. When possible, private bathroom facilities are an added blessing.

Try to give speakers the best of everything you have. Speakers are worthy of your best towels and linens, and their welcome basket can be larger and fuller. Try to have current magazines or books in the appropriate language in the room. Multiple Bible versions are helpful for study and message preparation. A good mirror, toiletry basket, alarm clock, iron, and hair dryer are appreciated.

SERVING SPEAKERS

Provide more services for speakers than you do for other guests. Offer to do laundry, ironing, and special food preparation. Freshen the speaker's room daily, replenishing supplies and emptying trash. Have a member of your hospitality team available for sightseeing tours, shopping trips, and chauffeur services.

Comments from YWAM speakers reinforce the importance of hospitality ministries. One speaker shared that when he spent a week in a foreign place, being left alone during meals was difficult, especially when surrounded by people with whom he couldn't communicate. However, human warmth, fellowship, bursts of laughter, and unforgettable special moments can redeem these situations. Another speaker said that he turns down some speaking invitations but travels at his own expense for others. He prefers to go where he has friendships, where people care about him and take time for him.

Many YWAM speakers return to a ministry occasionally or at regular intervals. It is helpful to keep a notebook or card file to record their special needs or preferences. One might need extra protein throughout the day; another only has toast and tea for breakfast. One doesn't eat the evening meal until after he teaches; another can't tolerate dairy products. You can also keep track of non-food preferences, such as an allergy to feather pillows or a need for blackout shades. If you make note of favorite treats or souvenir items, you can include them in future welcome baskets.

PREPARING FOR A SPEAKER'S ARRIVAL

Before a speaker arrives, promptly reply to any correspondence you receive. If it is the speaker's first visit to your ministry, send an information packet with a warm personal letter to acquaint the speaker with your ministry.

Be certain that you clearly understand the speaker's arrival plans. Communicate with anyone who might have contact with the speaker so that if he or she calls, pertinent information can be obtained.

Arrange for the speaker to be met at the airport or station. The person meeting the speaker should take special care with personal hygiene and attire. The host should be briefed about the speaker and his or her background and should be prepared to point out positive aspects of the country or city during the drive to the ministry.

Prepare the speaker's quarters using extra care, thoughtfulness, and attention to detail. Leave a speaker information packet in the room. This should include a personal welcome letter, base map, school syllabus, student and staff rosters (with photos if possible), class and base schedules, a list of other school speakers and topics, and a tentative schedule for the arriving speaker. It can be challenging for a visiting speaker to walk into an existing program without these items. Incidentally, this information is also helpful to local speakers and staff members not routinely involved in the school. A packet might be made available to the school staff for this purpose.

Provide generously for the speaker's nourishment and refreshment. Include fruit, breads, chips, crackers, pretzels, nuts, cookies, candy bars, and local specialties. Provide for hot and cold beverages, such as coffee, tea, hot chocolate, fruit juice, soft drinks, and bottled water. If there is a refrigerator in the room, stock it with cheeses, butter, milk, meats, and condiments.

RECEIVING AND SERVING A SPEAKER

When the speaker arrives at the ministry, he or she should be checked in with reception, giving any pertinent information required by the ministry. Warmly introduce the speaker to available ministry leaders, school leaders, and the hospitality team that will be serving him or her.

As you escort the speaker to his or her room, give a general orientation of the building or ministry. Make sure they know where meetings are held and meals are served. Offer to give a more complete tour later. Once the speaker is settled, ask any necessary questions about meal or schedule preferences. If you have a hospitality sheet, have them fill it out. See if the speaker has any laundry or ironing to be done right away. Share any peculiarities about the room or the facility, such as hot water usage or unusual noises. Finally, ask if you can do anything else to make the stay comfortable and invite the speaker to call the hospitality ministry at any time for assistance.

Often, a speaker will take breakfast in the room while preparing for a busy day of teaching. This option should always be offered. Take special care to arrange trays attractively, using a clean, colorful tray cloth and coordinating napkins. Add a small vase of flowers and a card. Prepare ample amounts of food, preferably serving what he or she has requested. Bring a hot beverage of the speaker's choice. Pick up the trays later.

Have someone escort the speaker from his or her room to the meeting room on the first day or two. If a vehicle is available for the speaker's use, make arrangements for its use. Ask if there are any particular people he or she would like to meet or have a meal with.

Respect cultural differences between your ministry locale and your visiting speakers. Culture shock should not be ignored; someone who has spent a week feeling culturally disoriented may be reluctant to return in the future. Take time to share local customs and routines while adapting to those of your speaker. Establish friendship with your speaker. Visit local areas of interest together. As your speaker becomes familiar with the surroundings and the ministry, oftentimes this helps with his or her speaking. A meal in a restaurant or a dessert at a sidewalk café may provide an unforgettable moment of fellowship for a foreigner.

When a speaker is about to depart, have someone go to the room and help carry luggage. It is nice if a familiar person can transport the speaker to the airport or station.

PODIUM HOSPITALITY

Determine who will provide podium and mealtime hospitality. In meeting rooms and dining halls, reserve a seat for the speaker, and designate a colleague to escort the speaker to and from meetings and meals.

Each speaker should have use of a podium set on a platform or floor section. Keep this area neat, clean, and orderly. Good lighting is crucial, whether it is overhead lighting or a small podium lamp. The podium itself need not be fancy, but it should be attractive and blend in with the room setting. It should provide a surface for the speaker's notes and room for a glass of water. Height and width of the podium should be proportional, and adjustable height is helpful. Stability is important, especially if a music stand is used to hold notes. With a music stand, provide a small side table to hold a water glass.

Decorations for the platform area can vary from existing everyday décor to special themed decorations for a particular event. Plants and flowers add a nice touch and bring life to the platform. Make sure that large plants or arrangements don't over-power a diminutive speaker. Other ideas include decorations that relate to a seminar topic, the speaker's home country, or the season. Care should be taken before each meeting to prepare the speaking platform or stage attractively and appropriately.

The hospitality ministry depends greatly on the technology team, so it is important for them to work together. Tech team members will be involved in setup, but hospitality workers should make sure cords are unobtrusive and taped safely out of the way. Provide the speaker with needed equipment, such as an easel, a blackboard or white-board, chalk or pens, and a projector.

If there is not enough room for chairs in the platform area, reserve seats in the front row. The podium should be in place, or nearby if it is to be moved into place after worship. During setup, adjust the podium height for an especially tall or short speaker. If musicians will be sharing the platform, make sure the front area looks balanced.

Prior to each message, place a pitcher of water and a drinking glass on or near the podium. Provide water for translators and musicians as well. Avoid using lightweight plastic or foam cups, which fall over easily. Provide enough water glasses for all speakers and translators. At a GO Festival in Randers, Denmark, there were twenty-four translators who were very appreciative of the water provided.

Before a meeting or teaching session, the speaker should be escorted to his or her reserved seat in the front of the room. Designate someone to provide a proper introduction of the speaker. This is both a courtesy and a way to convey information to the audience. In a corporate meeting, this should be done by the ministry leader, and in a school situation, the school leader should introduce the speaker.

INTRODUCING A SPEAKER

The introduction sets the atmosphere of the meeting and often determines how the speaker's ministry will be received. The person introducing the speaker should be articulate and expressive. Do not assume that everyone knows the speaker. In the introduction, include the speaker's name, correctly pronounced, and some personal information such as a brief background, a description of his or her ministry, and your relationship to the speaker or something else uplifting.

Once the speaker is at the podium, help adjust the microphone or podium height. When the speaker is comfortable, sit nearby in case you are needed to serve in any way.

Honoring one another is always a good practice. Find the best way to communicate honor to each recipient and anticipate how it will be received. Honor looks different for different individuals. People can be honored by recognition, words of affirmation, gifts, financial support, or by association with us. We honor because we value an individual.

"Be devoted to one another in love. Honor one another above yourselves. Never be lacking in zeal, but keep your spiritual fervor, serving the Lord. Be joyful in hope, patient in affliction, faithful in prayer. Share with the Lord's people who are in need. Practice hospitality" (Rom. 12:10–13).

guest speaker information sheet

Guest speakers are to receive total personal care during their stay, as if they were in your home. Please inform guest speakers that you would like to spend a few minutes with them, if possible, to learn how you can best serve them.

Guest _____

Host_____

Date(s) of visit_____

Guest room #_____

Guest of _____

Other information _____

☐ I have arranged transportation and assigned someone to pick guest up at airport/station.

☐ I have placed fruit, flowers, ministry information, welcome card, and name card in room.

☐ The guest room is neat and clean.

☐ For YWAM ministries, a copy of one of Loren Cunningham's books

(*Is That Really You, God?* or *The Book That Transforms Nations,* for example) and an up-to-date *Go Manual* are in guest room.

☐ Students' names and pictures are in the guest room.

☐ School syllabus and school schedule are in the guest room.

☐ Speaker has finalized copy of speaking/meeting schedule.

☐ Speaker is offered a beverage and snack upon arrival.

☐ Guest is asked if he or she would like to eat meals in guest room or in dining room.

☐ Guest is asked if he or she would like to eat with friends or students at mealtimes.

☐ The following records where and with whom a guest dines:

Date   Breakfast Lunch   Dinner

_____ _____ _____ _____

guest speaker hospitality checklist

Breakfast and cleanup:

☐ In guest room

☐ In hospitality room

☐ Hot food

☐ Cold food

☐ Both hot and cold foods

Preferred breakfast foods:

_____

Preferred breakfast time:

_____

☐ Escort speaker to classroom if necessary.

☐ Try to do breakfast cleanup during your first break from class.

Water on podium:

☐ Tray with pitcher of water and glasses for speaker and translator.

☐ Put out before the service or class begins, and have water in the glasses. (Lemon in water is a nice touch.)

During breaks:

☐ Tea   ☐ Coffee

☐ Milk? How much?

_____

☐ Sugar? How much?

_____

☐ Snack

Preferred snack foods:

_____

guest speaker hospitality checklist

Clothing care:

☐ Laundry ☐ Ironing

What time?

_____

Night check:

☐ Does guest need anything?

_____

_____

Daily room care:

☐ Replenish flowers

☐ Restock beverage cart

☐ Water flowers and plants, remove dead blossoms and leaves

☐ Empty trash

☐ Make bed

☐ Tidy up room

chapter 10

cross-cultural hospitality

CONDUCT YOURSELVES WITH WISDOM TOWARD OUTSIDERS,

MAKING THE MOST OF THE OPPORTUNITY.

COLOSSIANS 4:5 NASB

Working in Christian ministries, we are drawn to people and people are drawn to us. Even when we don't go to the nations, God will bring them to us. A wonderful part of the hospitality ministry occurs when we host guests from other cultures. Students come for training schools, lecturers come to teach, and travelers come to visit. Our creative God cleverly allowed for numerous peoples with different cultures to populate the earth. Just as small colorful tiles grouped together form a mosaic picture, many varying cultures interweave to create the interesting world we know.

Hospitality is a part of that big picture. It is a universal practice that can be effective in opening doors to friendship evangelism as well as relationships within the body of Christ. Ask God to open your eyes to the nations around you.

Recently an outreach team returned from Poland. One team member shared that the group's greatest evangelism tool during the outreach was a barbecue! The team members invited people to their temporary home, which happened to have a barbecue grill. While enjoying hamburgers with their Polish guests, they were also able to share the gospel and fellowship. That team understood the value of hospitality as a setting for friendship evangelism.

Cross-cultural hospitality can be a grand adventure. It allows us to experience cultures that are different from ours and to share our culture with others.

On the other hand, cross-cultural hospitality can be extremely frustrating if we are not prepared with an open heart and open mind.

God knew that people would be traveling from place to place and would need food and shelter along the way. He foresaw that many would relocate in foreign lands. Leviticus 19:33–34 gives insight into God's intentions for hospitality: "When a stranger resides with you in your land, you shall not do him wrong. The stranger who resides with you shall be to you as the native among you, and you shall love him as yourself, for you were aliens in the land of Egypt" (NASB).

Cross-cultural understanding is an art. It involves looking beyond what we find familiar and comfortable and what we take for granted. It requires an openness to adjusting and adapting to the words, phrases, nonverbal expressions, and comfort zones of others. Respect for other cultures is a necessity, even if we don't like some of their practices or routines. We must give people the freedom to be who they are.

THE BLENDED CULTURE OF HOSPITALITY

As we learn these differences and how to apply them to specific people groups, we can better understand our visitors. Specifically in the ministry of hospitality, it is our job to perceive our guests' needs and build bridges to span between cultures. Just as we should be prepared for them, we can help them to adapt to what we have to offer. Sometimes we need to help guests express their needs in a comfortable and familiar way. We need to "read between the lines" and really listen to what is being said.

No matter where they live, people want acceptance, respect, and fellowship. They appreciate beauty, peace, and a sense of territorial boundaries. What offends in one culture might be acceptable in another. In Europe, it is customary to make appointments to see one another; dropping in on someone is not common. Other cultures expect drop-in visitors and would never turn them away. In Africa, a chance meeting on the road may turn into a two-hour visit. In the United States, many people cannot spare more than a few minutes for an unplanned visit.

We should help build other people's confidence in their abilities whenever possible. In Uganda, when working with the local hospitality staff, I was often asked how to do certain things or how to handle specific situations because I was from the West. Before answering, I would ask other hospitality team members what they would do. Usually someone would offer a wise and sensible solution. I affirmed their responses and encouraged them in their decisions. I learned so much from the team there.

We all have strengths and weaknesses as individuals and as members of our culture. Allow grace and good humor to be your guide as you discover the joys of cross-cultural relationship.

In addition to differences in customs, food, homes, and surroundings, what is said, done, or served may mean different things in different cultures. Climate, availability, habit, hygiene, equipment, methods, and many other factors affect how things are done in each culture.

Some factors of hospitality vary from culture to culture, while other remain consistently applicable.

- Food is available and necessary in all cultures, though it will vary across the globe.
- Meal hours, length, and frequency may be different from one country to the next.
- Water is essential for survival, though in some areas, bottled water is advisable for health reasons.
- Rest and sleep are universal necessities, though beds range from floor pallets to four-poster beds, and bedding ranges from thin sheet blankets to thick duvets.
- Personal hygiene needs vary from country to country.
- Clothing depends on climate, custom, and availability.
- Arts and crafts are produced in most cultures, and markets around the world yield a wide variety of treasures.
- Home furnishings differ from culture to culture.
- Bathroom and dining facilities are all variables.
- Every nation has words for "welcome" and "thank you." The Internet makes it easy to learn these expressions for each guest you expect.

Understand the protocol of your guest's home culture. Find out how weddings and other special events are celebrated. What are his or her cultural traditions? How do people greet and introduce one another? Communicating about expectations is important as you expand your world across cultures. In many cultures, whoever suggests an outing is expected to pay for it. The United States is one of few cultures where it is typical for people to pay for themselves. However, money is a sensitive subject in many countries. In some cultures people pool their resources and share with the community. In others, individuals keep their money to themselves. In some nations the guest expects the host to make all the plans and decisions during their stay.

Cross-cultural hospitality may occur while we are in familiar surroundings or while we are immersed in a culture other than our own. Hospitality is certainly easiest in the comfort of our own home, with familiar foods, cooking equipment, household supplies, and furnishings. We can bless guests with our favorite meals and amenities, prepared the way we always have.

My family recently moved back to our home continent, and we miss cross-cultural living. But international staff members and students have a way of finding their way to our home. Being in an international organization is a privilege, and our lives have been enriched outside our own cultural setting.

If you're in a foreign country, enjoy its culture to the fullest and give your guests a taste of it too. Learn the special touches of local hospitality and pass them on to your visitors. In Hawaii, greet your guest with a lei. In Germany, have a special *Kaffeezeit* (coffee). A raclette meal would be appropriate in Switzerland, a *braai* in South Africa, and a *gyuvetch* (vegetarian casserole) in Bulgaria. Celebrating holidays as they do in other cultures is a rich experience. Our family still celebrates the Dutch *Sinterklaas*. It's very special to us.

As missionaries we are most effective when we learn about the culture in which we are living and share in the lives of the people. When we understand and participate in their lifestyle, we have a platform from which to share our own lives.

When Adele and Jim Noetzelman and their family arrived in Germany to work with small churches, many nationals were unsure of the sincerity of the American couple's commitment to them. But once Adele and Jim began taking language classes and enrolled their children in the local school, people who had watched them cautiously became confident that these foreigners really were serious about serving them. They began to open up to the family and encourage them with language help, cultural information, and pats on the back.

When in a foreign country, it can be fun to combine that country's culture with some touches from your homeland. That way, you can offer your guests the comfort of their own traditions while introducing them to some new ones. While some guests may balk at new foods, schedules, and accommodations, most will relish the opportunity to experience new things.

For example, when Adele served a visiting German man, he wanted to eat his customary bread and cheese breakfast each day. But he became very fond of American cheese and consumed quite a bit of it during his stay. When Adele prepared for the next family visiting from Germany, she stocked up on a variety of American cheeses. Alas, this new family had no interest in cheese; they were fascinated by the variety of American breakfast cereals. During their visit, they went through many boxes of cereal and gallons of milk, leaving the cheese in the fridge. Adele learned to be flexible, trying to have "a little bit of everything" on hand for guests.

Consider asking guests how to make one of their cultural specialties, if it is practical. Most visitors will be honored to prepare a dessert or a meal. Not only will it make your guest feel helpful and more at home, but it's also a great way to add to your international recipe file. Pavlova is a welcome dessert from New Zealand and Australia. Or ask a guest to prepare Mexican salsa, Indonesian satay, or Ugandan peanut sauce. Every culture uses special expressions of hospitality. Take advantage of YWAM's international style of learning from each other and sharing particulars of hospitality from various cultures.

A hospitality seminar in Switzerland had students from ten different cultures. Each student was encouraged to prepare a cultural favorite for a coffee break. Those ten-minute coffee breaks easily turned into half hours as students enjoyed learning about other cultures. One break featured Italian desserts of chocolates and pastries with small cups of Italian coffee. The Americans offered gooey brownies and decorated the coffee break table with real cowboy boots. From Holland came Dutch coffee served in Delft blue cups with *stroopwafel* (syrupy waffle cookies) melting on the top and flowers and candles decorating the tables. Croissants with jam and coffee surrounded a table with Swiss cowbells, Edelweiss, and candles. From the English, scones with jam and cream accompanied English tea served in real china cups. A feast of Danish almond pastries and smooth coffee was served on a table decorated with Legos. The Korean host decorated with orchids, prepared sushi and tea, and provided chopsticks. Cuckoo clocks adorned the table when a German black forest cake was served. A student from Mali displayed woven baskets and demonstrated a very special process of making tea.

Some traits are typical of certain countries. Indonesians always have time or make time for hospitality. Canadians are known as good cooks, and Italian hospitality is usually associated with food. In Belize, a visitor will always feel accepted, loved, and appreciated as a host takes time to visit. In Ghana, it is customary to walk guests to their cars after a visit. In Malawi, visitors are treated to special food.

Unfortunately, it is not uncommon for a person of one culture to accidentally offend a foreign guest. Misunderstandings occur because of language barriers, cultural expressions, or unfamiliar surroundings. It is helpful to learn as much as you can about various cultures, especially those from which you are expecting guests. Additionally, don't assume that guests are familiar with the culture of the country they are visiting. They may need your help navigating the customs of your area.

CULTURAL BASICS

Following are some basic cultural differences you may observe. These are generalities, not rules. In any country you will find those who are very unique individuals, who hear the beat of a different drummer.

- Americans send thank-you notes following visits, but other cultures commonly bring a gift on arrival.
- Europeans may eat bacon practically raw. Americans like it crispy.
- Serviettes and napkins mean the same thing in one country, and in another country they mean two different things!
- In America, the refrigerator is often considered "help yourself" territory. In European countries, no guest would dare to open it.
- Toilets in one country flush by pushing a handle; those in another flush by pulling a knob or string. In Holland, each toilet in a building may flush differently!
- American cooks and recipes use measuring spoons and cups. Other countries use pinches, shakes, or weight measures.

A collection of cultural information sheets may benefit your ministry. For example, a report on "Courtesies and Manners in Holland" covers basics on greetings (appropriate verbal expressions and physical contact), visiting procedures (bring flowers, shake hands with everyone), and eating and drinking (cue for beginning to eat meal, eat only what is offered). It also includes relationship dos and don'ts, and explanations of other manners and courtesies.

Start with an information sheet on your own ministry locale. This will be invaluable when students or visitors want to become familiar with the culture of your area. Understanding your own culture is imperative to communicating better with your visitors.

Colleagues and students from various countries can help you by providing information about other cultures. Accumulate as many details as you can. You and your team can review specific information before the arrival of your guests and be prepared to receive and treat them in a manner familiar to them.

A traveling speaker who has been away from home for a long time will be thrilled to be served a dish from his or her homeland. When Phil from England arrived in Uganda, I served him a quiche. He was so grateful to have something familiar to eat!

A visitor from a developing country may arrive with little or no spending money. The airfare may have taken all he or she had. Often nationals are not allowed to take cash out of their home country. If your culture requires cash, have some local currency available for your guests.

Food shopping and preparation in a different country may offer new challenges. We recommend that a cross-cultural host be prepared to measure by both English and metric methods. An American cook may want to travel with a small cooking kit that includes measuring cups and spoons, and the other way around if you are used to metric.

On my first trip to a Dutch market, I put up my fingers for two pounds of oranges. But the measurement in Holland was kilos, not pounds, so I carried five pounds of oranges on my bike ride home. With great laughter I quickly learned the metric system!

When you offer hospitality, you will be thanked in many ways. I remember some Japanese parents who bowed when I brought them pillows. You may be kissed on both cheeks, embraced, or offered another expression of thanks. When you honor the uniqueness of other cultures and extend the best of your own, you will be blessed by your guests.

Sometimes a language faux pas may lead to an embarrassing situation, especially if the language is tonal. But it's better to try the language and have some laughter than not to engage in it at all. (For more information on cultural diversity, read *Foreign to Familiar* by Sarah A. Lanier, published by McDougal Publishing.)

chapter 11

the role of the church

ACCEPT ONE ANOTHER . . . TO BRING PRAISE TO GOD.

ROMANS 15:7

OFFER HOSPITALITY TO ONE ANOTHER WITHOUT GRUMBLING.

1 PETER 4:9

Jesus instructs believers to actively show hospitality. Many churches have evangelism goals, and in today's society friendship evangelism is an important tool for reaching those goals. A lifestyle of evangelism is built on relationships, and being hospitable is one way to share the gospel whether you are in the church building or not. Hospitality and evangelism begin in the parking lot.

Hospitality is a ministry for everyone, not just for women. We are all created to contribute in many ways and put our gifts to work, and the ministry of hospitality is an invaluable way to contribute to a church. A team providing church hospitality can be very effective as they share ideas, put them into practice, and see events unfold. It is powerful when people allow God to express himself through them.

Jesus was a great role model in the area of hospitality. He ministered to all people, sat among them, and won their favor. Similarly, ministry takes place in various ways in church—from banquets and church fellowship times to small group settings, where intimacy is encouraged and people can grow in depth and authenticity. All are healthy ways for a body of believers to engage with one another.

In extending hospitality to the world, the church may be the only way a nonbeliever initially sees how the kingdom works. Hospitality in a church setting can be as simple as arriving early to unlock doors so visitors know that someone anticipated their arrival. But we also need to think about radical ways of being hospitable. That means going beyond our comfort zone and asking God for his vision of what hospitality should look like. (And it is always a good practice to honor with recognition those who quietly serve behind the scenes. Every church has them.)

Our responsibility to live out the ministry of hospitality should be taken seriously. It is our choice to accept others or not. Radical hospitality goes beyond the normal. How do we welcome others into our church? It's important to help people feel that they belong. It's not enough to welcome people; we must go one step further to incorporate them into the new setting. This could be as simple as showing a new mom where the nursery is located or inviting new people over for a meal. When we are radical, we are drastically different from the ordinary, and we go the second mile for our guests.

Never underestimate the power of your church greeters and ushers. Select friendly people for this role. Our family has moved to many new places and visited many new churches. We have often experienced stares instead of a warm welcome. On those occasions, our kids didn't want to visit again.

A pastor friend offers this great idea. Can you imagine a guest arriving on your church campus for the first time in the pouring rain and being greeted by members of the church's youth group armed with large golf umbrellas, smiles, and words of welcome? As the umbrellas are used to help folks stay dry until they make it to the sanctuary door, another group of people can meet guests at the door, take the umbrella, welcome again, and help guide them to the next step. If the family has small children, additional greeters can then take the family to the different children's ministry areas.

That's radical for a lot of churches.

Church settings can be diverse—from megachurches to home fellowships to villages—and hospitality will look different in each setting. Take your church locations and personality into account and ask the Lord what hospitality should look like. It is important to be in touch with your community, knowing how you can best serve in a quiet yet effective way. It may mean being in your local parade, or giving out water bottles on a hot day. Your church could have coffee or beverages available between several services on Sunday. Another simple gesture is greeter name tags; it's a helpful way for newcomers to identify them.

I remember a church we attended in Indonesia. We were invited to a meal after the service. While we were eating, our daughter Daniella started to choke on a piece of corn. She was turning blue when a dear elderly Indonesian woman appeared and helped dislodge the corn. To me this was radical: a stranger helped save our daughter's life.

We live in a new day, where visitors refer to church websites for information about worship services. Keep yours updated and current, with information on the programs you offer, childcare availability, worship style, and times of services. When a stranger arrives at your church door, live up to your website. At times the church has had an expectation that the pastor and his wife are the go-to couple for hospitality. Let's not put that unrealistic demand on our pastors; all of us are called to offer hospitality, especially if we are in leadership.

"Perfect" hospitality without a heart of love won't fly. Hospitality is a means of changing the world, and the church can participate by extending hands and hearts to reach out to individuals. When we engage in hospitality with a heart to bring love and acceptance, we may experience spiritual warfare. Recognize that, but proceed anyway! Hospitality counteracts the isolation, fear, and loneliness so prevalent in today's society, and it shows people how the kingdom of God works.

Offering hospitality for visiting missionaries and those who are home on furlough is a special role of the church. Hospitality contributes to keeping the vision of missionaries alive. Churches send out most missionaries, who serve on the front lines as an extension of the church. Having served as missionaries for many years, my family is grateful for our sending churches. They have ownership in our calling, they pray for us, and they financially support us. They gladly receive us when we come back to report what God has done through us with their support. It is a privilege to be an extension of a church body.

When your missionaries return home, be actively generous. Ask God what you can do to honor them. Some missionaries go without the things most people take for granted, and they are totally dependent on God for provision. A missionary is called to a life of responsibility, but most are not called to a life of poverty. They act out of obedience regardless of financial resources. Missionaries enjoy and appreciate the same level of hospitality we would give to a visiting pastor or evangelist.

Ask missionaries what they need or would like, and encourage them to make their requests known. Often they are hesitant to ask for things or request help.

Be observant and think of things missionaries might appreciate. Often families in the church are happy to provide them. Would baby equipment, camping equipment, a laptop computer, or a cell phone make the family's stay more comfortable?

One missionary recalls, "One summer our family of six returned to the US for a visit with church and family members. Our trip required a layover in a large city, and some generous friends gave us enough money to stay in a nice hotel overnight. Another friend offered to make the reservations for us, and we told him we would like to stay in a hotel near the airport. But after meeting us, he drove us to a halfway house operated by his church in a dark part of town. Even though we'd said we could pay for hotel accommodations, he thought any missionary would appreciate free lodging. We had a room in the gloomy basement with no lock on the door, and it was far away from the toilet. After my husband left for a speaking commitment, I spent an uncomfortable evening trying to juggle the bathroom trips of three children and diaper changes of a toddler. As the night wore on, the hallway became noisy with activity. The next morning I wanted desperately to wash my hair before flying home, but we could not find a shower or warm water. A cold-water hair rinse in a small sink was all I could manage. Though we appreciated our friend's heart to serve us, that evening put a damper on our trip home."

Whether they stay with a family or independently in a guest apartment, your visiting missionaries may appreciate services such as grocery shopping, laundry, play dates for their kids, and transportation. Most churches and ministries have members who love to serve in this way. When returning home for a visit, many missionaries enjoy checking out favorite places they left behind and seeing all the changes that have taken place. A basketful of local information, brochures, maps, gift cards, a community newspaper, and even cash would be a warm and helpful way to welcome them. Encourage church or ministry members to invite missionaries into their homes. Be aware, though, that a furlough or itinerating schedule can fill up quickly with meetings, business and medical appointments, and time with relatives and close friends. Suggest gatherings of friends and small groups so that missionaries can touch base with several people at one time. Often a large number of acquaintances and people interested in meeting the missionaries can be hosted at the church or ministry location.

When missionaries return from the mission field and set up housekeeping again, the church can offer hospitality by helping them furnish their new household (or even providing a furnished home). Some groups take up a collection so missionaries can purchase what they need. Others ask for a list of desired items and collect them for the missionaries. Find out whether an item is a gift or if it is on loan with an expected return time. Be sensitive about the quality of what is offered. Often missionaries are given unwanted items that have little use left in them. One family received a rusty old washing machine that had been left outdoors. It operated, but not very well, and visits to a laundromat proved to be more efficient.

The heart of Jesus glowed through a woman named Sharon when she delivered a recliner chair to a missionary family who was getting reestablished in the US. Sharon had ordered a new recliner for her living room and intended to give the family her old one. But before she loaded it into her truck, she felt an inner voice urging her to give the missionaries the new chair. She did, and the family was extremely touched. They'd been given many used and worn items to set up their home; something fresh and new was a blessing. Sharon was equally blessed to have given her best.

Hospitality can take another form—that of a package sent to missionaries on the field. It is special for missionaries to be remembered on birthdays and holidays, and a care package is a great way to express appreciation for a particular missionary. Be generous and think of things from home that the missionary may miss. One Christmas when our family lived in Europe, we received a box full of American goodies from our supporting church. It felt like opening a treasure chest! It was heartwarming to watch our children discover microwave popcorn, boxed macaroni and cheese, and Oreo cookies.

Years ago, five days before leaving to serve in an African nation for an extended time, my husband and I discovered we were expecting a baby. I quickly unpacked my usual clothes and filled my suitcase with new maternity clothes. Later, our co-workers thanked me for honoring them by wearing new clothes when I arrived. They said most people come to minister in old clothes, and they know that is not how most people dress in their country of origin.

One of our African pastor friends advises, "When you are from a developing country and you are receiving missionaries from the West, receive them without expecting something back. Don't see the missionary from the West as a door to your support, or your passport to the Western world. Hospitality is choosing to give with an offer of a cup of water or tea, with no intention of getting something from the one you are receiving."

As believers we can be very effective when we walk in obedience to the voice that speaks within. We shouldn't go beyond our means; however, we can give generously in obedience. Let's spur one another on in our church settings to be generous with the resources that our gracious heavenly Father has given and equipped us with. Let's be intentional in our hospitality. Let's reach out to that new family in church, invite the visiting pastor home for a meal, or love on our missionary families. Lives will be changed and pointed toward the kingdom when we walk in love and generosity toward God's people.

every great event

ON THE THIRD DAY A WEDDING TOOK PLACE AT CANA IN GALILEE.
JESUS' MOTHER WAS THERE, AND JESUS AND HIS DISCIPLES HAD
ALSO BEEN INVITED TO THE WEDDING. WHEN THE WINE WAS
GONE, JESUS' MOTHER SAID TO HIM, "THEY HAVE NO MORE
WINE." . . . JESUS SAID TO THE SERVANTS, "FILL THE JARS WITH
WATER"; SO THEY FILLED THEM TO THE BRIM. THEN HE TOLD
THEM, "NOW DRAW SOME OUT AND TAKE IT TO THE MASTER OF
THE BANQUET." THEY DID SO, AND THE MASTER OF THE BANQUET
TASTED THE WATER THAT HAD BEEN TURNED INTO WINE.

JOHN 2:1–9

There are three phases of involvement for any event: preparation, the event itself, and the cleanup. Of the three, preparation consumes the most time and energy. Prayer is a vital part of the preparation phase, and God's grace is essential in planning any event. The word of the Lord is a foundation to fall back on. When crises arise or plans don't turn out the way you expect, God will be there.

PREPARATION

This begins with planning. Basic considerations are facilities, food, and program. First, know why you are planning the event and what purpose it should accomplish. Know your target audience and who will attend. Decide what kind of atmosphere you want. Will it be elegant and formal, or casual and cozy? How will you decorate and what theme and colors will you use? What food and beverages will you serve? Consider traffic flow—how should the room be set up? How many chairs or tables will be needed? Guests will mingle longer if there are fewer seats. How long do you want people to stay? What cultural needs or expectations will the guests have? Will any guests need overnight accommodations?

How many people will it take to plan and prepare for the event? Assign all parts of planning to capable individuals, starting with your hospitality team. This is when it is crucial to know how each one handles stress and pressure; pair up your people accordingly. Other people such as staff or students can be recruited to help as well. This is a great opportunity for creativity in teamwork. Link up those who will work together in the same areas. Be specific with assignments and expectations, including deadlines. Delegate as much activity as possible. Focus on loving people. And keep thorough records of all planning, activity, and results for future use.

1. Assign a host or hostess for the event, and arrange crews for decorating, cooking, program, facilities, and cleanup.

2. The designated event coordinator should meet with each group to go over the plans. Stay in close contact with the head cook and anyone else involved with the evening. Make sure all supplies are on hand for decorating and serving. Don't forget parking availability, traffic flow, and other logistics.

3. When planning menus, look outside for inspiration. If the weather is warm, consider outdoor picnics and barbecues. On cold days, think about indoor fondue, pasta dishes, or warm menus suited for the season.

4. Once all the jobs have been covered, set a schedule for preparation. Have each person and committee do as much as possible ahead of time. When planning a timeline for event preparation, leave the last two or three days open for final details, additions, or changes.

5. When decorating for an event, pay special attention to the room's entrance, which will set the tone for the gathering. Consider the type of lighting desired and the seating arrangements. Think about table decorations and special touches that will add flair. For a large event where paper goods are used, station trash cans in suitable locations. Add a special touch of a candle or a sprig of flowers in the bathrooms and make sure they are clean and have ample toilet paper, soap, and towels.

6. Arrange tables to allow for adequate walking space between them. Each table should have a centerpiece (as simple as a candle or single flower), a filled set of salt and pepper shakers, serving utensils, and a beverage pitcher. If coffee or tea will be served, add creamer and a sugar bowl.

7. Assign one server to every two tables. Have a few extra servers to fill in the gaps and help the other table servers. If serving buffet style, servers should be standing by to assist guests and pour beverages.

THE EVENT

As the event is taking place, don't fret if you forget something or if an idea doesn't turn out as planned. If there's time left, pray for a solution or a substitute. If not, just have a good time and enjoy your event. Others will too.

During my first YWAM outreach, our team had a special meal known in YWAM as a love feast. We prepared a delicious meal of lasagna, arranged fun decorations, and planned a wonderful evening. We were just sitting down to eat when I realized that I'd forgotten to buy beverages! I told the Lord that I had nothing for our guests to drink. "Help me," I said. "What should I do?" I decided to put out pitchers of ice water with lemon slices. This was fine, but I wished I had planned more carefully. Five minutes later, an employee of a local fast food restaurant appeared at the door with two gallons of root beer, just to bless the YWAM team. God provided the drinks for our celebration, and it was the best drink we could have served that evening!

CLEANUP

This is a standard chore, so do what needs to be done. Have teams to work in the kitchen and in the other rooms, taking down decorations and returning the rooms to their normal condition.

Step back and analyze your event. What went well, and what would you do differently? A follow-up debriefing session is helpful for team members to discuss their conclusions.

There are many keys to successful events. Pray for a heart to serve at each one. Let God be God, and give him his rightful place in your plans. He wants to be in the details. Our worldview is much more limited than God's. Time and money need not hinder us. God wants us to ask him for resources; he is not poor and neither are we. He blesses and multiplies as we offer what we have and let him do the rest. Know Jesus intimately, and believe in what he can do.

Remember that people are more important than plans. A celebration is a way to honor guests. Allow each event to become something special. Think about such details as formality, time, program, childcare, invitations, and menu. Consider the cause for celebration. For communion, keep bread and juice or wine on hand. Honor staff members on their birthdays. Wedding and baby showers, which are American traditions, can be celebrated in other cultures as well. Don't be afraid to do things with flair.

Keep all important parts of the event in front of you, always looking at the big picture. Do your best, and keep your mistakes to yourself. Catch them quickly and make changes to correct them. Faith grows when we don't always have our ducks in a row.

Use what you have available to create a pleasing atmosphere. Draw a diagram of the room if that helps you picture it. Focal points might be flowers, the head table, or a podium. Use lamps and candles to augment room lights. Borrow live or silk plants, ornaments, and other items from other locations or homes. Use natural items like twigs and rocks. Be specific with color: blue could mean baby blue, navy, or dusty blue. Use space to your advantage. High ceilings may be lowered with sheets.

Enjoy the day! Take time to celebrate, relax, and have a good time yourself. Take special care with those individual expressions that have meaning to you—your colors and personal touches. Never turn away help; use all the help that comes your way. Don't limit event planning to a few people. Involving many people gives honor and ownership. Build a team that complements your weaknesses, and empower your team to use their gifts. Always have examples to reproduce, especially table settings, for the team to refer to when setting up. Have an event kit ready—a box containing scissors, fishing wire, thin wire, duct tape, transparent tape, and tacks. Clean up as you go.

One of the joys of YWAM is the fun we have at our special events. Whether it's an impromptu casual get-together or a well-planned formal event, we love to get together. We have great fellowship, eat fun food, and often celebrate a special occasion.

Every culture has its own traditional celebrations, which should be a part of YWAM life in that culture. But we also introduce new events from the backgrounds of our broad range of staff members.

Every ministry hospitality team should be prepared for last-minute parties by keeping a supply of snack foods, beverages, and decorations on hand. A hospitality team can creatively make something wonderful out of any impromptu celebration.

Once you have prepared as well as you can in whatever time you have, be relaxed and flexible. Be like a duck: calm and serene to the eye, even if paddling like crazy under the surface!

In Kona, Hawaii, the Cunninghams' lanai was the site of many large gatherings. Often as we were putting the last flowers on the tables and lighting candles, drops of rain would begin to fall. Darlene and I would literally pray back the storm clouds, and I can't remember a single time when the rain didn't abate. God listened and answered our prayers.

PARTY THEMES

Use your imagination when planning parties around various themes. In addition to celebrating a ministry's unique culture, consider special interests of staff members or students, seasonal themes, or favorite books or characters.

A Chronicles of Narnia theme was chosen for a love feast at Lakeside, Montana. Décor was based on the book series, and guests entered through a wardrobe door into a room full of snowflakes, candles, and white tablecloths. The walls were strewn with character figures and Narnia quotes. Testimonies and dancing at a "palace" ended the evening.

It is always good to take time to play together as a community. In Lausanne, summers were filled with barbecues on the lawn. In Hawaii, barbecues took place on the beach. A day of fun together in Uganda included games, music, and food. In Montana, ice hockey and roasted marshmallows were shared on a winter day.

WELCOME NIGHT

Many YWAM ministries host a welcome night for groups of new students or staff members. Either light refreshments or a meal may be served. It is great fun to decorate and serve food typical of the base locale.

In Lakeside, Montana, that means decorating the cafeteria to look like a log house. The menu is barbecued beef on buns, and the meal is followed by a square dance. Newcomers to YWAM Kona are welcomed with a Hawaiian luau featuring a pit-roasted pig. Island Breeze, a dance team from YWAM Kona, provides entertainment and a historical Hawaiian presentation.

Lausanne staff members in native costumes serve Swiss cheeses and delicious chocolate in an atmosphere of the Switzerland countryside, complete with alpenhorns.

Plan a short program of introductions, base information, and a get-acquainted mixer game for welcome nights. If you have many foreign students, an introduction to the culture and language is also helpful.

COMMUNION

There are many ways to observe communion today, including using individual cups and crackers or shared glasses and a loaf to tear apart. The blood of Jesus may be represented by grape juice or wine, and the body represented by bread or crackers.

The hospitality team should always be prepared for communion, which is often a spontaneous event. Many times I've been caught off guard and had to run and gather the elements, but it's easy if you have them readily available.

Keep bread, juice, and cups on hand, according to your base's communion customs. Your needs should be met by a supply of small cups or large goblets, grape juice or wine, and small crackers or loaves of bread (keep some in the freezer). A corkscrew will be needed for wine bottles. If goblets are shared, pass a cloth napkin with each glass so the rim may be wiped after each sip. These items should be labeled "for communion only" and set apart from items for everyday use.

Allow one liter of juice or wine for every twenty-five servings. Eight people can usually share a full goblet. One cracker per person should be offered; servings per loaf of bread will depend on the size of the loaf.

INTERNATIONAL NIGHT

One of YWAM's strengths as a mission is its international emphasis. During most terms in Lausanne, about twenty nationalities were represented. Our ministry offered wonderful opportunities for learning about different cultures. Hosting an international night was one way of doing this.

Staff members decorated the tables and provided food that was representative of their own home countries. On one such evening, the following nations were featured: Australia (pavlova), Holland (butter cake), Indonesia (satay with peanut sauce), Ireland (tea bread), Korea (sushi), Mexico (fresh salsa and chips), Nepal (chai tea), Norway (fruit soup), Thailand (spring rolls), Uganda (ground nuts and pineapple), and Ukraine (borsch).

International Night offered an incredible evening of tasting new foods, learning ethnic dances and greetings, and praying for one or more of the nations represented.

"I cried at the end of International Night—I loved it!" one student reported. "It was an inspiration and reminder of how much God has burdened my heart for the nations."

Another student added, "I loved this night! It was done really well. In fact, it almost convinced me to be a full-time missionary!"

OPEN DAY

Open Day or Open House at your ministry is an opportunity for your local community and ministry to get acquainted. An understanding of your ministry can go a long way toward acceptance from your neighbors. It's also a way to show appreciation to your local supporters.

Planning can be quite simple. Offer tours of the ministry, written and spoken information about the ministry, and refreshments. Use cultural sensitivity when planning refreshments. Include foods customary in the local community, as some people are hesitant to try unfamiliar cuisine.

Have plenty of outgoing staff members available and ready to greet visitors, lead tours, and answer questions about your ministry. Tour guides should be articulate and knowledgeable about the facilities. When possible, greeters and tour guides should be nationals, and bilingual if appropriate. These individuals should receive a strong orientation early in the week to prepare them for the duties of the day.

BIRTHDAYS AND ANNIVERSARIES

As a ministry, we are a family. Birthdays are opportunities to celebrate life, and anniversaries recognize the joy of marriage. Each person should be honored in some way, whether your custom is an announcement with cheers or a cake with candles. Be aware of cultural customs. In South Africa, the twenty-first birthday is extremely important and specially celebrated. Posting a calendar of birthdays and anniversaries allows staff and students the opportunity to extend personal greetings all day long.

CHILDREN'S PARTIES

Plan parties and special meals with children in mind. Even though they are included in many of the ministry's special events, it is fun to have a party just for the youngsters once in a while. They can even help with planning and preparation. They are in tune with what their peers enjoy, and their involvement is a great way to teach creativity.

BRIDAL AND BABY SHOWERS

Weddings and new babies give us special opportunities to bless others. Again, we play the role of family and close friends by planning celebrations of these happy occasions.

In some cultures, showers are part of these celebrations. Wedding and baby showers are a special North American tradition where a party is given for a bride or a new baby and they are honored with gifts.

Staff members can give small social events like showers; it is not necessary for hospitality to actually host each one. However, it is best if the hospitality team ensures that a shower is given for each bride or new baby.

Be aware that showers are not familiar to some cultures. Although Americans know them well, in England they are uncommon. In Australia and New Zealand, communities sponsor teas for brides.

WEDDINGS

Weddings are typically family affairs, hosted in most cultures by the family of the bride or groom. Since most YWAMers are far away from family and lifelong friends, we often become family for these occasions. The hospitality team can take the place of the hosting parents by helping the engaged couple plan for the wedding and carry it out. The entire ministry can be involved, creating a very special celebration.

Preparing for a wedding involves many of the basic principles of event planning. However, some special considerations should be made for housing and transportation of family members or friends who come for the ceremony. If the number of overnight guests exceeds your accommodations, you may need to ask friends of the ministry if they would be willing to host visitors. Be considerate of the cultures of both guests and hosts when making housing decisions.

When possible, family members of the bride and groom should be given rooms at the ministry rather than with neighbors. If you have unoccupied speaker accommodations at your location, it is a nice gesture to house the bride's parents there.

Visiting family members and friends of the bridal couple should be treated as special guests. Be sensitive to their cultural needs during their visit and concerning the wedding. Designate specific individuals to act as personal hosts. These hosts should be prepared to offer a tour of the YWAM ministry to the visitors and help them plan any shopping and touring excursions.

A staff member who is gifted in this area should act as wedding coordinator, overseeing plans and wedding day events. This person should be emotionally removed from the bridal couple to be able to make decisions and spot problems.

The coordinator and a member of the hospitality team should sit down with the bride and groom to plan the ceremony and reception. Decide on the location, officiate, time of ceremony, seating, decorations, photography, music, transportation, food, reception program, and other details.

Once decisions have been made, the bride and groom should decide who will do what at the wedding and reception. Let them personally ask those people to help. This includes not only their attendants but also the reception servers and other helpers. For the duties of the hospitality department, one or more individuals should be assigned to meet each need. Two or three hosts should oversee the reception and receiving line. Assign cleanup crews for the wedding and reception sites. Don't limit yourself to the hospitality department; recruit help from the entire ministry or church family.

Encourage the bridal couple to relax and avoid stress during the days before their marriage, while the hospitality department takes care of the details. The parents of the bride and groom, if in attendance, are likely to be feeling many different emotions. They may feel like outsiders as they watch "their" responsibilities carried out by strangers. Be sensitive, warm, and supportive of them. If the parents desire to contribute to the preparations, respect their wishes to be involved and allow them to help.

GRADUATIONS

A major cause for celebration is when YWAM's University of the Nations (U of N) students earn their degrees. It is a huge moment for the students who have accomplished this major goal. YWAM founder Loren Cunningham says that the testimonies shared at these graduations are like paychecks for the staff. It is wonderful to hear about the students' growth and their experiences.

As more students complete their education at the U of N, YWAM will be having many more graduations. Unlike many YWAM celebrations, the graduation commemoration is a formal event that is well planned and involves much thought and prayer.

Written programs are an important part of our graduation ceremonies. Each student is listed, as is the order of events for the evening.

Following the actual ceremony is a reception to honor graduates. It may be elegant and simple or extravagant, whatever the Lord directs. The hospitality team is usually responsible for the reception. They may also be asked to decorate or plan other aspects of the event. Know what role your department will play, and then follow through to the last detail. The food may be as simple as cake and beverages, but as a tribute to the graduates, the atmosphere should be special.

The decorating theme for the evening should honor and symbolize the culture of the particular university campus. Lovely woven baskets and fabrics could represent a graduation in Africa. Beautiful music and colorful flowers would create an elegant atmosphere for a European graduation. For a graduation in Hawaii, each guest presented leis to the honorees, and some graduates were adorned with twenty or more leis! For a graduation in Uganda, two goats were butchered for the occasion. What a feast we had! It was a whole day of celebration.

FAREWELLS

In ministries and in many churches, we are constantly importing and exporting people. Good-byes are never easy, but they are important for closure and for commissioning. Each departing staff member and outreach team should be recognized in some way. Keep note of when people are leaving so that no departures will pass unnoticed.

A farewell can be as simple as gathering to pray for the person or group, or as elaborate as a party. Special prayers and words of affirmation and encouragement are always appreciated, especially those in writing, which can be read over and over. It is appropriate to have different types of sendoffs for long-term and short-term members, but it's wise to set standards for each category and be consistent. The most important factor is that no one is overlooked.

LOVE FEASTS/BANQUETS

The YWAM love feast was initiated in the early days of the mission. It was usually held each weekend, at the end of a long week of work. The feast was planned as a time set apart to marvel and reflect on God's goodness. University of the Nations provost Tom Bloomer explains that the Hebrew Sabbath meal was the inspiration for the love feast idea, which was common in New Testament days and became a ritual in the eighteenth century Moravian Church. "For a Jew, the Sabbath meal is not just a meal, and not just a nice meal. It is the preparation for the Messiah. You get your house ready, you put on your best clothes, you have the best food, and you're waiting for the Messiah."

Today love feasts remain important to YWAM for the same reasons. Students and staff enjoy them immensely. It is a time to draw away from ministry to focus on fellowship and reflect on God's goodness. YWAMers describe love feasts as "being a family," "expressing appreciation to each other and to the Lord," "celebrating God's faithfulness," "highlight of the week for entertainment and fellowship," "time to establish relationships and enjoy each other," and "a time of fellowship and bonding." Love feasts may also be a time for reaching out to guests.

When guests are invited to love feasts, amazing things can happen. The early Lausanne love feasts were open to visitors from the community. "I don't think we ever had one love feast without guests," recalls Tom Bloomer. "It was always all the staff, all the students, and some guests from outside YWAM. We actually had a waiting list of people wanting to come to one of our love feasts."

A special meal and some type of program should be included as part of the love feast. Many love feasts begin with worship, a teaching or message, and/or Bible study. Communion may be included. Program possibilities include a departmental or cultural presentation, outreach team report, children's music or drama performance, or group folk dancing. Impart variety into your love feasts and use different themes, programs, and menus.

When I lived at YWAM Heidebeek in the Netherlands, we had a love feast every Friday night. Everyone loved coming to sit together in a lovely environment and sharing testimonies about what God had done in our lives that week. With candles and fresh flowers on the tables, the setting was always *gezellig*, which means "cozy" in Dutch.

One love feast was a barbecue at the beach. It could have been a colorful fun atmosphere, but I forgot to create the tone. What could have been simple turned into a disaster for me. Just buying paper tablecloths and putting some thought into the total effect would have saved the day. But I learned from my mistakes.

God multiplied the food for me during one particular love feast when I underestimated people's appetites. We had a group of businessmen from Asia, and I cooked a very American meal. The only thing left over was the rice. They enjoyed the meal so much everyone wanted a second round. To my amazement, the bowls just kept getting deeper.

Where did YWAM get the inspiration for these wonderful gatherings called love feasts? YWAM teacher Tom Bloomer tells the history:

OUR YWAM STORY: LOVE FEAST BEGINNINGS

In 1971 at YWAM Lausanne, there were a couple of serious accidents on Sunday afternoons, notably sledding accidents. When Loren and Darlene Cunningham sought the Lord for the reason, they understood Him to say that there needed to be a new commitment to His holiness, especially concerning Sabbath observance, and then He would restore His protection.

One other key influence during the same period was the visit to the Lausanne base of two women from the Evangelical Sisterhood of Mary in Darmstadt, who loved YWAM but were surprised at the unruliness of the meal times (people jumping up to get things, shouting across the room, and reading their mail at the table). They told Loren and Darlene that their meals were times of peace, quietness, and relationship.

When we came as students in 1974, one of the first teachings in the school was that a meal could and should be an ordered time of fellowship. We were taught to stay seated for a full forty-five minutes, to enjoy the meal and fellowship with people around us, and to give priority to one another at the table.

In 1971 Reona Peterson-Joly returned from London, where she was pioneering YWAM England and supporting herself by teaching in a school for Orthodox Jewish children. When Reona heard that the leadership was studying what the Lord meant by Sabbath observance, she shared what she had understood from the Orthodox Jewish families.

To sum up, the house was cleaned from top to bottom to purge it of leaven. There was no work on the Sabbath day. The Sabbath began on the eve of the day with the best meal of the week, which meant the best china, the best food, and the best clothes for the family. Most of all, there was a total focus on the Lord.

Another key influence at that time was Joe and Judi Portale's return to the base after visiting believers in Czechoslovakia with Al and Carolyn Akimoff. Arriving at the house of a Czech elder on Christmas Eve, they participated in a love feast that consisted of passing round, flat bread around while telling what each person meant to them and how they loved them. In this way YWAM first heard about this 250-year-old Moravian tradition, and that's how we began to use the term "love feast."

Loren and Darlene Cunningham proceeded to study the relevant passages in the Word (Isaiah 56 and 58, among others) and to restore the Sabbath by adapting some Jewish traditions to YWAM Lausanne:

- No work on Sunday, so the noon meal was usually cold (salads and sandwiches prepared the day before to reduce kitchen work).
- No sports or hard play. Not a legalistic rule, but an outworking of the commitment to "turn your foot from doing your own pleasure" on the Sabbath (Isa. 58:13 NASB).

- The Sabbath was a day of quiet, rest (many took naps), walks in the forest, and concentration on the Lord. (Of course, there was church in the morning and the main weekly community gathering in the evening too.)

To prepare for the Sabbath, we had a love feast the evening before, on the eve of the Day of Rest. We moved the tables from the crowded dining room into the larger lecture room to have space for all students and staff to sit down together, and to have room for guests as well. The tables were beautifully decorated with candles, centerpieces, and flowers. The best meal of the week was prepared, everyone dressed up, and we set out place cards so people wouldn't always sit next to their same friends.

There was a sense of expectancy and holiness throughout the day, with a commitment to spiritual preparation. In the afternoon, students and staff prayed for hours for the love feast. People knocked on each other's doors to confess things to one another and ask forgiveness. Nobody wanted to be an obstacle to the Lord's meeting with us in the evening, and each one took that responsibility seriously. One message that Loren preached several times in those years was "The Sin of Achan" from Joshua 7, about how one person's sin could stop the flow of the blessing of God in the community.

The children had their own special meal with decorations, but it was earlier so they could be put to bed and the parents could be free to fully participate in the love feast.

When everyone arrived for the meal, they waited together so all could enter the lecture room at one time. The joy and expectancy was high, with people in their best clothes, wondering whom they would be seated with (especially the singles).

During the meal, all remained seated except one group that served. Each week a different group took that responsibility. Sometimes there were special songs and music, but it was all oriented toward worshipping the Lord.

At the end of the meal, the love feast leader gave a meditation from the Bible on one aspect of the character of God. After the meditation, we went into a time of worship while still seated around the tables. Anyone could lead out in prayer, read a passage of Scripture, or start a song, as the worship wasn't directed from up front. The worship lasted at least an hour, or sometimes two. Time seemed to stand still, and no one wanted to leave. We waited on God together, in His presence.

In other words, it was not just a horizontally but also a vertically oriented meal. When the Lord's Sabbath is honored and His people commit to holiness, He makes Himself present in an unforgettable way.

From Lausanne, the love feast spread to other YWAM bases. In 1974 the Cunninghams took love feasts to Hawaii, and the concept went around the YWAM world.

The love feasts were a tremendous amount of work. The hospitality crew spent most of Friday preparing the tables. Just folding the napkins took ten people a full hour after lunch. As base leader, I took all of Friday afternoon to prepare the meditation for the love feast, to prepare myself, and to pray for the evening. We even prayed about the seating, and which singles to seat together. Later we switched the love feast to Friday evening and took Saturday as a full day off.

In more recent times, "love feast" has come to mean any meal that's different from the normal ones. For example, the love feast we attended at one base consisted of a buffet and everyone sharing in a social, rather than spiritual, experience.

We saw the fruit of the love feasts over the years. These gatherings were one of the only times that all of the staff and students, with a few outsiders, met with each other and with God. Sometimes guests made commitments to the Lord after being there with us.

As late as 1974, we didn't know how to worship; we just had "singing." But in YWAM Lausanne, we learned to worship God during the love feasts. We had many fun nights, skit nights, mime nights, and costume nights during our school in Lausanne in 1974. In fact, we averaged at least one skit per day, and a "no-talent night" every three weeks. Most bases could use more of these kinds of evenings; they're tremendously important in community building.

But let's not call them love feasts. Because throughout the history of the church, that term has meant a community meal; one which is lived in true fellowship and in the presence of the holiness of God.

Loren and Darlene did a great job adapting biblical and Jewish traditions to the hippieish, Jesus-movement YWAM culture of the early 1970s. Now we need someone to re-adapt them for postmodern youth. What could a love feast look like for twenty-somethings? It should be different from what we had going in Lausanne, but should still include the emphasis on beauty, fellowship, solemn joy, and the holy presence of God.

Take the time to plan something that is better than ordinary. I will never forget an event at the Plaza of Nations at the Kona, Hawaii, YWAM base. The Plaza, which includes a fountain and flags from around the world, is a place of inspiration. We decided to host an evening dinner there with thirty guests. As we planned the event, our imaginations took off, and we had an incredible evening of food, entertainment, and fellowship just as the sun was setting. The event went off without a glitch and was a night to remember.

event planning checklist

Keep the big picture in mind:

☐ Catch mistakes quickly and make necessary changes

☐ Keep your head clear to make good decisions

☐ Relax and enjoy the event yourself

☐ Keep good records of all planning and activity

☐ Enjoy the people you work with and believe in them

☐ Know each person's responsibilities and sphere of decision-making authority

☐ Review past events: what worked well and what needs to change

☐ Know your audience or guests

Things to consider:

☐ Dates and times

☐ Program content

☐ Facilities

☐ Food

☐ Transportation

☐ Budget

☐ Program schedule

☐ Deadlines

☐ Registration procedures

event planning checklist

Confirm:

☐ Audiovisual

☐ Food

☐ Transport

Promotion: brochures, posters

☐ Review progress

☐ Run special event

☐ Keep an overall perspective

☐ Solve problems, make decisions, and encourage staff

☐ Make yourself available

☐ Check on staff

☐ Bring closure and debrief

☐ Pay accumulated bills as necessary

☐ File records for next event

banquet checklist

Love feasts are important social functions. They first took place when YWAM began, as a time to draw away from ministry. The purpose of a love feast is to spend time in fellowship and reflection on the Lord's goodness. Any banquet can be planned in a similar way.

☐ Check to see who will be in charge of program and if there are any special plans.

☐ Pray about theme, colors, décor, program, dress, and menu.

☐ Meet with those in charge to discuss plans.

☐ Create a menu with your kitchen coordinator.

☐ If the love feast will not be held at your location, reserve facilities early.

☐ Decide what colors and decorations you will have and begin to prepare them.

☐ Contact audiovisual department for overhead microphones.

☐ Let everyone know what to wear to the event.

☐ Designate a setup team, a serving team, and a cleanup team.

☐ Gather tablecloths, napkins, vases, candles, place settings with cutlery and glasses, filled salt and pepper shakers, beverage pitchers, and centerpieces.

☐ Decide on room setup, with tables arranged neatly and space to walk between tables.

☐ Reserve seats for special guests and those in charge of event.

☐ Fold napkins and assemble centerpieces.

☐ Meet with servers before the meal to pray and give instructions.

☐ Assign one server per table and a few extra helpers to serve up the meal in the kitchen.

☐ If second servings are available, determine size of portions.

wedding checklist

Appoint two coordinators to oversee the wedding ceremony and two or three hosts to oversee the receiving line and reception.

Things to consider:

☐ Guests

☐ Housing for incoming family and guests

☐ Transportation for family during their visit

☐ Social planning

Ask the bride and groom to pick a friend or someone from hospitality to help their guests sightsee. Encourage the couple to remove pressure and to keep in mind the stress level of the early planning stages and the week before the wedding. Even in the best family situations, there is the built-in tension of wanting everyone to have a good time. Be sure to have someone from hospitality spend time with family and friends by sharing about the ministry and giving a tour. Many guests may have never seen the setup and know very little about your ministry.

Ceremony:

☐ Minister

☐ Location of ceremony

☐ Time of ceremony (consider season and weather, and have an alternative plan)

☐ Decorations: who will head this up and size of crew needed

☐ Seating

☐ Music (person responsible for music and equipment)

☐ Transportation for bride, groom, family, and guests

☐ Transportation of equipment

☐ Movement of flowers, chairs, and furniture from wedding area to reception area

☐ Cleanup

wedding checklist (cont.)

Reception:

☐ Time

☐ Location

☐ Food

☐ Decorations

☐ Seating: sit down? buffet? wedding party served at table?

☐ Receiving line: who will be in it, where it will be

☐ Emcee and program

☐ Gifts: what to do with them

☐ Toilet facilities

☐ Cleanup

Keep flow of people moving before and after ceremony and during the reception. Do not leave guests unsure of what to do and where to go.

small event checklist

Things to consider:

☐ Formal or informal?

☐ Indoors or outdoors?

☐ Buffet style or table service?

☐ Special instructions from person requesting event:

_____

_____

_____

_____

_____

_____

_____

_____

_____

_____

_____

_____

_____

Helpers:

Name   Phone number

_____

_____

_____

_____

_____

☐ Time of event

☐ Menu

☐ Food

☐ Dessert

☐ Beverages

☐ Food prep

☐ Set up chairs, tables

☐ Tablecloths

☐ Table decorations

☐ Set table

meaningful mealtimes

THEN JESUS SAID TO HIS HOST, "WHEN YOU GIVE A LUNCHEON

OR DINNER, DO NOT INVITE YOUR FRIENDS, YOUR BROTHERS

OR SISTERS, YOUR RELATIVES, OR YOUR RICH NEIGHBORS. . . .

BUT WHEN YOU GIVE A BANQUET, INVITE THE POOR, THE

CRIPPLED, THE LAME, THE BLIND, AND YOU WILL BE BLESSED.

LUKE 14:12–14

One of the most important qualities of sharing a meal is the atmosphere. It should be one where God's love and presence are felt. The atmosphere can be enhanced by things that express creativity and are arranged with love. Each one of us has been endowed with different gifts and talents; dare to be creative in your own style!

When we host guests, it is not our intention to put on a display but to focus on simplicity and the service of delicious food. Using a touch of creativity at mealtime reflects many aspects of our Creator. What could make a meal more charming than a fresh and attractive table and a menu carefully planned with colors and textures in mind?

MEAL PLANNING

What may start as a simple meal can lead to a grand time from start to finish. Eating is much more than nutrition for the body; it is also food for the soul. God created a variety of foods with many colors, textures, shapes, and flavors. We should consider beauty and variety in the meals we serve. Keep nutritional value in mind when you plan meals. Take care not to overload guest meals with calories.

Plan meals and shop for nonperishables ahead of time. This will take away the last-minute jitters. Make a list of guests, what will be served, and what groceries are needed. Write out a schedule of when each step of preparation must be done. Consider room and table décor and atmosphere. And give the occasion to the Lord, asking that his Spirit will be present at your special meal.

Creating a friendly atmosphere is important in meal planning. Here are some tips:

- Make sure your entrance is clutter-free and welcoming.
- Match your table settings to the event, whether formal, informal, or picnic style. You can do a wonderful variety of things with your tablescapes and settings.
- Think through lighting, especially in the evening as the natural light turns to darkness.
- Remember that people will move around. Think through traffic flow and arrange furniture to accommodate this.
- Music is a wonderful addition. It enhances a welcoming entrance, and quiet music makes a good background for a party. Keep the music low so people can hear their conversations.
- Remember, you can burn the meat, drop the flowers, and be late with dinner—but people will still have a good time if you love them and have fun. Be able to laugh and be flexible. Love your guests and take good care of them. Smile, look into their eyes, and tell them how happy you are that they've come. People do respond. Advance preparation sets the stage for a happy gathering. Place cards are a great way to ensure that talkers are seated next to good listeners. If you're trying to get new people acquainted with others, place cards can help facilitate this.

Food was part of the message Jesus so vividly conveyed in the word: turning water into wine at the wedding feast, multiplying loaves and fishes by the Sea of Galilee until all were satisfied, and the breaking of the bread and sharing of the cup.

Sometimes partaking together does not involve a full meal. A simple beverage and an attentive ear will honor a stranger or friend. Whether serving a cup of tea in Asia or a ginger drink in Africa, a beverage is an invitation to stay a while, sit and refresh one's body, and share the latest events in one's life. In India, offering a cup of tea symbolizes accepting and identifying with another.

Often women who don't have kitchens available come to cook meals in my kitchen. Once my friend Millie from Africa asked for these ingredients: a few tomatoes, onions, beef, beef gravy, collard greens, and cornmeal. I wondered her dish would taste like. It was delicious—one of the most amazing meals I have ever eaten.

Include some dishes in your menu that most people enjoy, and perhaps one or two side dishes that are unique to your culture and may be new to your guests. Depending on the occasion, meals may be as simple as soup and bread or salad and fruit, or as elaborate as a large buffet with numerous main courses and side dishes.

For large crowds, plan main dishes that taste good at any temperature. Even food that starts out hot may have cooled by the time the last person is served. Chicken and ground meat casseroles are good choices; other foods don't taste their best unless served hot. Avoid dishes that require last-minute attention, such as gravy made from the roast drippings, as large quantities are difficult to make in a hurry.

It is better to have leftovers than to be stuck without enough food. Generally, men and teenagers eat more than women and children. To ensure that the main dish will feed everyone, serve the portions yourself or place it last in a buffet line. Plan generously so no one goes away hungry, and allow for unexpected guests.

On one occasion, a ladies' luncheon at Darlene's home was interrupted when Loren came in with several men and asked if there was enough food for them to have lunch too. We had no sooner finished serving them when the Cunninghams' son, David, came home with friends and the same request. We had three luncheons that day instead of one!

Balance the color, texture, weight, and seasonings of food. Avoid monotone menus, such as white fish or chicken served on a white plate with rice, cauliflower, and bread. Balance heavy foods with lighter fare, and finish a spicy meal with a light, refreshing dessert. Climate makes a difference too; people generally prefer light and refreshing foods in warm weather and heavier, hot foods when the temperature drops.

Avoid trying out new recipes on guests. A failure may bring added stress, which a host doesn't need. Work within your capabilities, and prepare what you feel confident about. On the other hand, don't be afraid to try new things when requested to do so.

The first person I served in YWAM hospitality was a man named Graham Kerr. At the time, I didn't know who he was other than a speaker I was to serve for the week. When I asked him what he'd like for breakfast the next morning, he requested poached eggs.

I knew I would need help, as I had never cooked a poached egg. Since poached eggs are my dad's specialty, I called and asked him how to prepare them. He gave me very clear instructions and then asked who my visitor was. When I told him, Dad said, "He's a famous cook!" I hadn't known that my guest was a chef with his own televised cooking show, *The Galloping Gourmet*.

I hardly slept that night, and I included the Lord in my dilemma by asking him to help me cook poached eggs in the morning. I poached those eggs, and they turned out well! Imagine impressing the Galloping Gourmet with poached eggs. I was grateful to the Lord for my dad's instructions. Since then the Lord has become intimately involved in my work in hospitality, answering many prayers.

Keep your pantry and freezer stocked to simplify your meal planning. Sometimes you can even prepare an impromptu meal with what you have on hand. For light meals, have snacks, desserts, coffee cake, cookies, and cakes ready to be served at a moment's notice. In a pinch, be creative about using what you find in your kitchen.

One particular evening at YWAM Kona, guests arrived unexpectedly, and I asked myself, "What am I going to make them for dinner?" I looked in the refrigerator and surveyed the variety of leftovers, wondering how I could make a meal from them. In his mercy, God inspired me with some ideas for preparing and presenting some nourishing and tasty dishes. With extra touches of fresh flowers on the trays and ice cubes in the beverages, the previously plain food looked very appetizing. My guests were blessed to be served such a lovely meal.

As we give out of nothing, God will do the rest. Since then, I've learned to keep food in the freezer and pantry for unexpected guests. But it is comforting to know that if I'm caught short, the Lord will come through.

SIMPLE MENU IDEAS

Breakfast (serve coffee and tea with each menu)

- Scrambled eggs, ham rolls (ham slices spread with cream cheese and rolled up), toast, butter, jam, fruit
- Cheese omelet, bacon, bread, butter, jam, fruit or juice
- Hard cooked eggs, ham rolls, yogurt, juice, hot chocolate
- Fried eggs, bacon, fruit, toast, butter, jam
- Fruit flavored yogurt, bread, butter, jam, sliced cheese, juice
- Pancakes or waffles, butter, syrup, bacon, fruit
- Cold cereal, milk, sugar, sliced fruit, sweet rolls, juice
- Hot oatmeal, milk, sugar, honey, raisins, fruit, juice

Bread meal

- Sliced fresh bread
- Assortment of spreads and toppings: butter, soft and hard cheeses, peanut butter, apple butter, cottage cheese, lettuce, tomatoes, cucumbers, sprouts, other raw vegetables

Salad meal

- Mixed greens
- Assorted toppings: hard cooked eggs, chopped or sliced vegetables, slivered meats and cheeses, nuts, sunflower seeds, croutons, variety of salad dressings
- Bread, muffins, biscuits, or breadsticks

Casserole meal

- Main dish casserole
- Vegetables, salads, fruit
- Bread

Soup meal

- Main dish soup
- Raw vegetables, fruit
- Bread or rolls

GUIDELINES FOR PREPARING AND SERVING A MEAL

Allow enough time (at least two hours) to prepare and serve so you need not rush. Find out details: Where will the meal take place? Who will be the guests? How many guests will be served? Will it be formal or casual?

- Decide on the menu.
- Prepare the food.
- Check the bathroom and clean it or pick up as needed.
- Tidy up the room where the meal will be served. Dust table and chairs. Arrange correct number of chairs around the table.
- Choose appropriate dishes, cutlery, glasses, place mats, napkins, and center-pieces.
- Take one plate to each place setting; center it and put the cutlery, napkin, and drinking glass in place. Set the lower edge of the place mat flush with the edge of the table. Place the plate and cutlery 1 in. (2.5 cm) from the edge. Place drinking glasses above the tip of the knife.
- Prepare the beverage and pour it into a serving pitcher. Chill it in the refrigerator.
- Check ice supply; keep plenty of ice on hand when you serve beverages.
- Put the following food items in appropriate serving containers and place them

on the table: salt and pepper, salad dressing, butter, jam, honey, and tartar sauce. Place a butter knife or serving spoon next to each dish as needed.

- Pick or purchase flowers for the centerpiece, parsley and other garnishes for the plates, and mint for the dessert as needed.
- Set out dessert plates, dessert forks or spoons, coffee cups and saucers, and small coffee stirring spoons. These should be ready to be used right after the main meal is cleared. Ice cream desserts can be prepared beforehand and stored in the freezer. Prepare most of the dessert beforehand, if possible, to avoid a rush at the last minute.
- Fill cream and sugar containers.
- Fill coffee maker so it's ready to be turned on just before serving the meal. Be sure tea bags are available.
- Put ice in the drinking glasses and fill them just before the guests arrive.
- Turn on dinner music.
- Take a moment to pray and serve in a peaceful, relaxed, and pleasant manner.
- After grace, serve the plates from the left of each guest.
- Refill beverage glasses from the guests' right.
- While guests are eating, complete preparations for the dessert.
- Clear plates and silverware from the right (never rush). Also clear salt/pepper, butter, rolls, and salad dressings.
- Place cream and sugar on tables.
- Give each person a clean dessert fork or spoon.
- Serve dessert from the left and coffee or tea from the right.
- Refill coffee and tea.

  If guests are staying a while after dessert is eaten:
- Clear dessert dishes.
- Offer more coffee and tea.
- After guests have left, clean up.

More tips for serving

- Serve hostess first. She will take the lead, which makes the guests comfortable.
- When pouring coffee at the table, pour coffee in the cup, and then serve the cup to the guest.
- British people usually prefer tea to coffee, and they use cups and saucers, not mugs.
- Be sensitive to how many calories you are giving the guest.

Tips for buffet service

- Buffet centerpieces can be quite tall, as guests will be standing.
- Matched china is unnecessary for a large crowd.
- Displaying food at different levels makes your buffet table look interesting.
- Think through the buffet setting before guests arrive. Allow adequate space, and determine the proper place for each serving dish in advance. When a dish requires two utensils for serving, allow enough space between serving dishes for guests to set a plate down.
- If possible, serve beverages at a separate table.
- Allow adequate space around the buffet table for guests to move comfortably.
- Situate small tables near enough to each guest if there is no main dining table.
- Ask guests to stand for grace if they are seated when dinner is announced.
- After grace, give instructions for food service.
- If guests hesitate to approach the buffet table, graciously ask a specific individual to begin. The others will follow.
- Service the buffet table regularly, and refill serving dishes as necessary.
- When all guests have been served, extend an invitation to those who wish to return for more.
- Clear dinner plates from the eating area as guests finish. Dessert may be served on the buffet table.

buffet tables

Round table

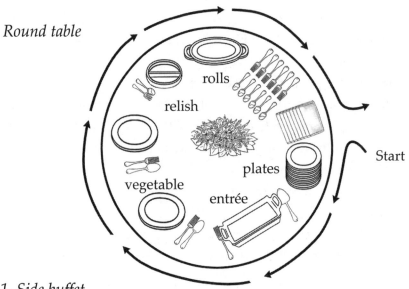

rolls

relish

vegetable

entrée

plates

Start

1–Side buffet

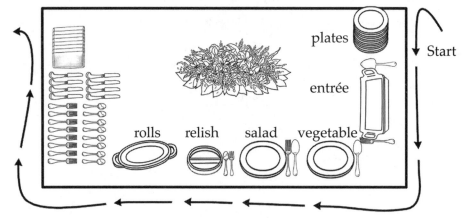

plates

Start

entrée

rolls   relish   salad   vegetable

2–Side buffet

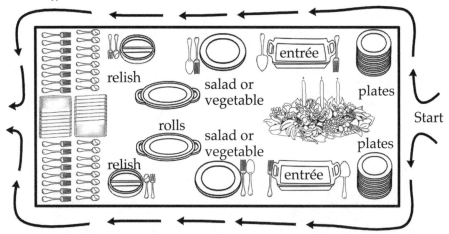

relish

salad or vegetable

entrée

plates

rolls

salad or vegetable

Start

relish

entrée

plates

table settings

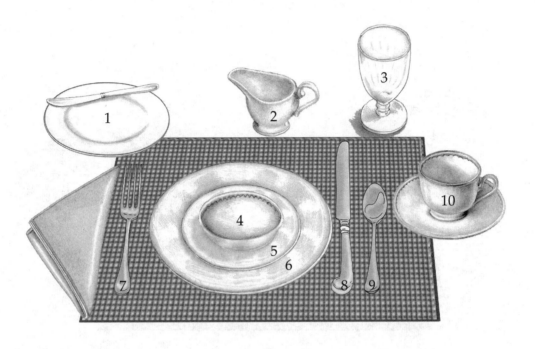

Breakfast table setting

1. toast plate

2. syrup pitcher

3. water glass

4. fruit bowl

5. fruit bowl saucer

6. service plate

7. fork

8. knife

9. teaspoon

10. coffee cup & saucer

table settings

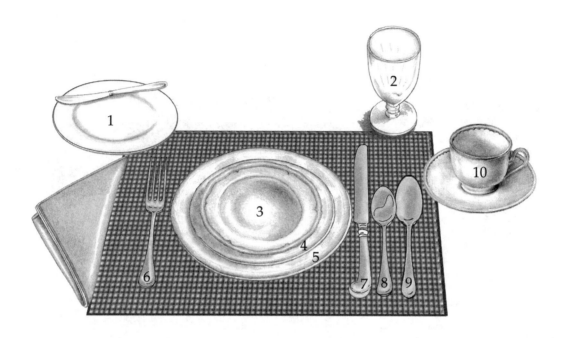

Luncheon table setting

1. bread plate

2. water glass

3. soup bowl

4. soup saucer

5. service plate

6. fork

7. knife

8. teaspoon

9. soup spoon

10. coffee cup & saucer

TABLE SERVICE

Once guests are seated at a table and are ready to be served, take a moment to pray and be calm. You may wonder if the vegetables are crisp enough, what happened to the parsley, or how the meal ended up being all white! But you have done your best, so relax and enjoy serving your guests.

Serve food from the left and beverages from the right. Serve women first, beginning with the hostess, and then the women to the hostess's right or left. The men are served next, ending with the host. With multiple tables, complete one table at a time.

Remove dishes from the right. As dinner plates are removed, take the butter, salt, and pepper as well. When you are ready to serve dessert, add sugar and cream for coffee or tea.

TRAY MEAL SERVICE

When arranging a meal on a tray, it can be a challenge to find room for everything. Think through dishes, glasses, and cutlery. Include all necessary items without making the tray look cluttered. Small containers and pitchers will help make everything fit.

Give the guest enough to eat, especially protein foods. Arrange a small garnish on the plate. Add salt and pepper, a napkin, and perhaps a flower in a tiny vase. Minister to the spirit by adding a small scripture card to the tray. If you have to walk far to deliver the tray, warm the plate before filling it. Cover the tray with a towel so the food will remain warm. Remember to pick up the tray after the meal.

TABLE DECORATIONS
Table coverings and décor

- Coordinating tablecloth or runner, placemats, and napkins (paper or cloth)
- Place cards, formal or informal, at each place setting
- Any type of napkin ring to dress up paper or cloth napkins

Centerpieces

- Basket of fruit
- House plants
- Single flower blossoms floating in pretty bowls
- Several candles of different heights
- Simple vase with fresh flowers, especially unusual varieties
- Ideas for taper candles: Carve the stem end of a pretty apple or tiny pumpkin with an opening the size and shape of the candle. Carve deep enough to hold the candle securely.

napkins

Lily

1. Unfold and lay napkin flat. Fold corners in to center.
2. Hold corners in center, flip upside down, and fold outside corners to center again.
3. Hold center, flip right side up. Open up corners and slip glass into center. Carefully pull up corners and turn out to create petals.

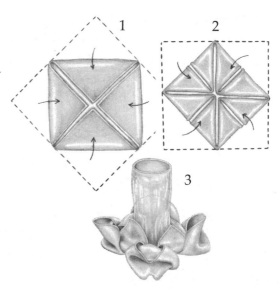

Americana

1. Fold napkin into quarters.
2. Fold bottom and sides to center.
3. Fold in thirds.
4. Slip inside the napkin ring.

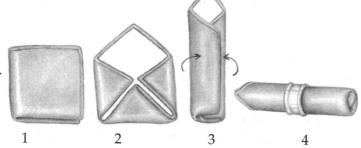

Weisbaden

1. Fold stiff-style napkin in half, diagonally.
2. Fold up 1.5" (4 cm) from seam.
3. Pleat into 6 accordion pleats.
4. Slide 2 compressed pleats between each pair of fork tines.

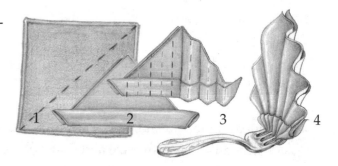

napkins

Fan

1. Fold napkin in half.
2. Pleat into 1" (2 cm) accordion pleats.
3. Slip end into glass and spread out.

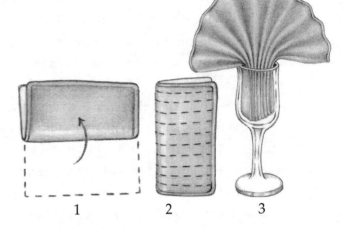

Standing fan

Pleat as in step 2 of the Fan, but only up to 4" (8 cm) from the top.
1. Fold in half with pleats outside.
2. Fold loose corner down and tuck in.
3. Carefully lay napkin crease side down on plate, allowing to open.

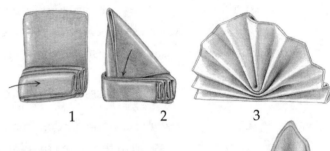

Scarf

1. Fold into quarters.
2. Visualize pleats.
3. Fold in half and pleat each half.
4. Slip inside the napkin ring.

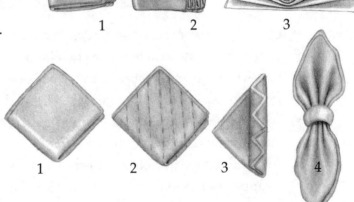

Open house

1. Start with step 1 of Scarf, folded again diagonally. Fold sides to meet at middle.
2. Fold under bottom points.
3. Fold back on middle crease.
4. Position on plate and pull up points. (May secure underneath with clip.)

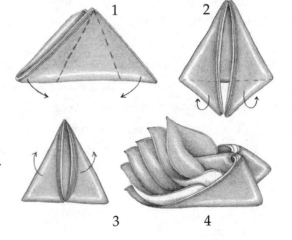

The thoughtfulness expressed by flowers is a distinctive way of telling your guests that they are special. When decorating with flowers, a single blossom can be very effective. In Uganda, it was often a challenge to find flowers that would last for any length of time. One particular afternoon, I was almost ready to give up when I spotted a gardenia bush. I picked a blossom and a few leaves and put them in a small dish. Even that little arrangement added a personal touch and enhanced the room with its wonderful fragrance. However, avoid highly scented flowers on a dining table, as sometimes the scent affects how the food tastes.

In the Netherlands, we planted a flower garden for the use of the hospitality department. It was a fun project with the added bonus of many fresh flowers available for our use. I often used orchids or anthurium flowers in Hawaii, because they usually stay fresh for about two weeks.

Use your imagination to discover flower containers among your household items. A vase or bowl can be placed inside a basket or box. Flower heads can be floated in a clear glass or crystal bowl. Keep your eyes open for other additions for floral arrangements. While flowers or greens will be the central focus, natural objects such as rocks, shells, driftwood, and interesting twigs can add a finishing touch.

Professional tips for flower arranging

- Carry cut flowers from the garden in a heads-down position.
- To reduce decay, strip the stems of all foliage and thorns that will fall under the vase's water line. To enhance water intake of woody stems, pare the bottom two inches of bark away and pound the stripped portion before plunging in water.
- To prevent sap from escaping, sear the ends of hollow stems. Insert a stick to strengthen weak hollow stems.
- To condition the flowers, lay them flat on newspaper and wrap. Plunge the wrapped bunch into tepid water for 3 to 5 hours or overnight.
- Proportion an arrangement to the table it will decorate. Keep the arrangement low if people will be sitting around it.
- To prolong freshness, spray the arrangement with tepid water morning and evening.
- To repair the bent stem of a heavy-headed flower, insert a toothpick through the center of the blossom and into the stem.
- To revive wilting flowers, snip off 1/2 in. from stem under water, and plunge into a deep container of water.
- When trimming a brown spot along a leaf margin, shape the leaf to resemble its original proportions.

FOOD PREPARATION AND COOKING HINTS

Do as much of the preparatory work in advance as you can. In YWAM we work with what we have available, compromising and making do when necessary. At some locations we cook with just the basics; at others we have a wide selection of cooking equipment. A well-equipped kitchen might include the following:

- Salad spinner for quickly drying salad greens and garnishes
- Food processor for chopping and slicing
- Knife sharpener to avoid dull blades
- Thermal carafe for storage of hot beverages
- Slow cooker for hot cider, mulled wine, gravies, sauces, soups, or stews
- Large stainless steel mixing bowl for salads, ice, or punch
- Large serving platter for meats, hors d'oeuvres, or pasta
- Large serving spoons for ladling
- Serving trays for transporting used dishes back to kitchen
- Attractive plastic cups in case you run out of clean glassware

When possible, cook in a kitchen that you are familiar with. Your meringue or cookies may not turn out the same in a strange oven. Bake a practice run with anything delicate. Ask someone who is familiar with a range or oven what its idiosyncrasies are.

The following tips come from YWAM hospitality seminar participants, who are from many cultures.

- For light and fluffy omelets and scrambled eggs, beat in 2 T. water for every two eggs. The water turns to steam and lightens the eggs.
- When cooking eggs in the shell, add a teaspoon of salt to the water to avoid cracking.
- Hard-cooked eggs peel easily when cracked and placed in cold water immediately after cooking.
- If soup tastes too salty, a raw piece of potato placed in the pot will absorb the excess salt.
- A tablespoon of cooking oil or margarine added to the water for cooking pasta will prevent boil-overs.
- Remove the tops of carrots before storing. Tops drain the carrots of moisture, making them limp and dry.
- Vegetables that grow underground (potatoes, beets, carrots) should start off cooking in cold water.
- Vegetables that grow above ground (peas, beans, greens) should start off cooking in boiling water.

- To get walnut meats out whole, soak the uncracked nuts in salt water overnight before shelling.
- To avoid soggy piecrusts in chiffon or cream pies, seal the baked crust before filling as follows: Brush the still-hot baked pie shell with slightly beaten egg white, covering all fork-pricked holes. Then add filling.
- When rolling out cookie dough, sprinkle board with powdered sugar instead of flour.
- To freeze frosted cookies, place them unwrapped in freezer for two hours, then wrap. They won't stick together.
- If whipping cream looks as though it won't whip, add a few drops of lemon juice and a pinch of plain gelatin powder.
- Cakes and other desserts can be neatly cut with the proper knife and cutting techniques: For angel food cakes and quick breads, use a serrated knife. For meringue desserts and cake rolls, use a knife with a thin, sharp blade, and wipe the knife with a wet cloth or paper towel after each cut. For layer cakes, use a well-sharpened chef or French knife. Cut cakes with a sawing motion and a light touch to avoid smashing the cake.

Baking tips

- Always preheat oven as directed. Before heating oven, make sure racks are in correct positions. Generally, yeast mixtures and pastries should bake toward the top of the oven, cakes and cookies should be placed in the center, and meringues should be cooked on the lowest shelf possible.
- Keep oven door closed during the first 15 minutes of baking. The exception is for small cookies, which may be checked after 5 minutes.
- To prevent shrinking, leave cheesecakes and cream cheese cakes in the oven to cool after baking. Turn off the oven and leave the door open until the temperature inside the oven is at room temperature.
- When you need only an egg yolk for a recipe, lightly beat the white of the egg and freeze it in a small jar or freezer container. When thawed, use as fresh egg white for meringues.
- Ice cream scoops are great for making uniform drop cookies and filling muffin cups. Use small scoops for cookies.

Rescue baking disasters

- Crumbly cookies: Crumble the remainder and add coconut, rolled oats, and cinnamon. Use as topping for fruit or serve as a dessert with cream.

- Overbaked cookies: Crumble in food processor or blender, use for crumb crusts.
- Broken or crumbled cake: Cool, then crumble large pieces. Cover pieces with enough sweetened condensed milk to mix into a pudding. Or make a trifle (sponge cake), using custard or prepared pudding instead of milk. Place in a bowl, leave to set. Top with chunks of gelatin, whipped cream, and nuts.
- Leftover or stale cake: Use for trifle as above. Or fry in butter and serve with fruit and cream. Or crumble and mix with a beaten egg and melted butter to moisten well. Bake 30–45 minutes at 350°F/180°C. Serve warm with custard or cream.

GARNISHES

A simple garnish can make any plain food look more attractive and appetizing. Simple edible garnishes include sprigs of herbs, whole small fruits, and molded butter. Fruit and vegetable slices, cutouts, curls, twists, and other shapes are also attractive. Edible flower blossoms make beautiful garnishes for salad bowls, cake plates, and other serving dishes. In Europe and North America, try pansies, nasturtiums, violas, and carnations, all of which can be safely eaten. In tropical areas, orchids work well and look lovely.

Garnishing tips: Ice water may be used to crisp or freshen vegetable and fruit garnishes. A saltwater solution of 2 tablespoons salt to 1 pint of water makes vegetable slices pliable. Lemon juice prevents darkening of fruit slices.

garnishing with fruit

Sugar-frosted grape garnish

Clean small clusters of plump, ripe grapes. Combine one slightly beaten egg white with 2 tablespoons of water. Brush the grape clusters with the egg white mixture. Sprinkle with sugar and place on a wire rack to dry at room temperature for several hours. Be very cautious to keep everything clean as contaminated egg white can lead to salmonella poisoning (eat right away, refrigerate for later, or discard after use as a decorative garnish).

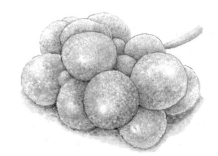

Strawberry fruit fans

Take a ripe, fresh, unblemished, and clean strawberry. Set the strawberry stem side down on a cutting board. With a small, sharp knife carefully cut several slices into the berry without cutting all the way through (A). Prepare all the berries you need. Store on paper towels and cover in the refrigerator until needed. To finish, lay the berry on its side. Gently twist the slices, spreading like a fan (B).

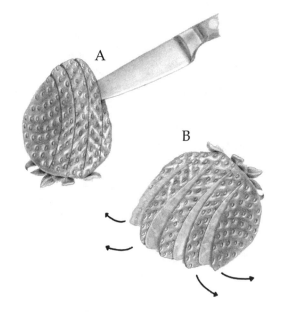

gourmet pineapple cuts

Pineapple boat

1. Cut pineapple and crown in half.
2. Using a curved, serrated knife, cut the fruit from the shell. Don't cut through the shell.
3. Cut the fruit into pieces. Place pieces (and other fruit if desired) into the shell.

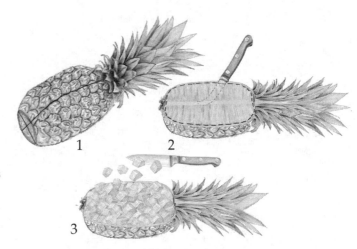

Pineapple spear cut

1. Cut off top and bottom.
2. Cut away outer shell strip by strip.
3. Cut diagonal grooves to remove "eyes."
4. Cut vertical spears from the fruit. Slice spears crosswise to make smaller wedges.

Outrigger canoe cut

1. Quarter pineapple, leaving the crown on.
2. Cut fruit from the shell with a curved knife.
3. Remove core and slice fruit crosswise into sections. Arrange neatly on shell.

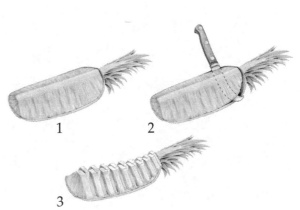

recipes

Here are some favorite recipes that I have gathered from friends around the world. They have been tested and tried, and all of them are fantastic!

Abbreviations: in. = inch, cm = centimeter, tsp. = measuring teaspoon; Tb. = measuring tablespoon; pt. = liquid pint (.5 liter).

BREADS, CAKES, COOKIES, AND DESSERTS

scones

European measurements	Cup measurements
8 oz. self-rising flour	$1^{1/2}$ cups self-rising flour
1 tsp. cream of tartar	1 tsp. cream of tartar
1/2 tsp. bicarbonate of soda	1/2 tsp. baking soda
1/2 tsp. salt	1/2 tsp. salt
$1^{1/2}$–2 oz. butter (or lard)	3–4 Tb. butter or shortening
1/4 pt. milk	2/3 cup milk

Preheat oven to 425°F/220°C. Lightly butter a baking sheet. Sift flour, cream of tartar, bicarbonate/baking soda, and salt into a bowl. Rub or cut in the butter, working it into large flaky crumbs. Stir to a soft dough by mixing in the milk with a knife. Roll dough out to a thickness of 1/2 in./1 cm and cut into rounds with a 2–$2^{1/2}$ in./5–6.5 cm diameter biscuit or cookie cutter. Arrange on a baking sheet fairly close together. Powder tops of scones with flour. Bake for 12–15 minutes, until scones rise and turn golden. Serve hot or cold. Can reheat in the microwave for a few seconds. Serve with jam and cream.

oliebollen

(a type of doughnut served in Holland on New Year's Eve)

1 envelope active dry yeast

3 Tb. sugar

1/2 cup lukewarm milk, scalded

2 eggs, well beaten

$1^{1/2}$ cups lukewarm milk

optional: 1 cup currants

1/2 tsp. vanilla

1 tsp. salt

4 cups flour

2 cups seedless raisins

3 apples, peeled and diced

Soften the yeast for 10 minutes in the 1/2 cup scalded lukewarm milk with the 3 Tb. sugar added. Mix this with eggs, $1^{1/2}$ cups milk, vanilla, and salt. Beat in flour gradually. Add raisins and apples. Cover bowl and let rise $1^{1/2}$ hours. Drop by heaping teaspoonfuls in hot cooking oil. Turn if necessary. Some balls will turn by themselves while cooking. Remove from oil with a straining spoon. Sprinkle with powdered sugar while still hot. Serve hot or cold. Makes five dozen.

chapati

(a type of bread made in East Africa and India)

2 cups whole wheat or white flour

1/2 tsp. salt

1/2 tsp. salt

7/8 cup water

Combine flour and salt in a bowl. Stir in margarine and water. Mix well to form a soft dough that can be kneaded, sprinkling in an additional 2 Tb. water as needed. Knead well; cover with a damp cloth and set aside for one hour. Knead again. Break into golf ball-sized lumps, roll into balls, and roll each ball out on a floured board to 1/4 in.–1/2 cm thick. Dust each chapati lightly with flour.

Heat a heavy ungreased skillet. Brush skillet with melted fat or brush each side of chapati with melted margarine before frying. Fry two minutes on each side or until lightly browned. Keep chapati warm and puffy by placing directly on lowest rack of oven at 200°F/90°C until ready to serve.

pancakes

1¹/⁴ cups flour	2–3 tsp. baking powder
1 Tb. sugar	1/2 tsp. salt
1 egg, beaten	1 cup milk
2 Tb. oil	

Mix ingredients together. Ladle onto a hot, greased frying pan or skillet; turn over after a few minutes.

lemon bread

1/2 cup shortening or butter	1 tsp. baking powder
1 cup sugar	grated peel of 1 lemon
2 eggs, slightly beaten	1/2 tsp. salt
2 cups flour	1/2 cup milk
3/4 cup poppy seeds	

Glaze: 1/4 cup sugar and juice from 1 lemon

Cream shortening and sugar. Add eggs. Sift together flour, baking powder, and salt. Add to sugar mixture with milk. Add poppy seeds and grated lemon peel.

Bake in a greased medium-size loaf pan at 350°F/180°C for 1 hour. For the glaze, combine 1/4 cup sugar and juice from lemon. Poke holes in the bread with a fork and drizzle glaze over the top.

boterkoek

(Dutch buttercake)

2/3 cup butter	1 egg, beaten
1 cup sugar	1¹/² cups flour
1 tsp. almond extract	1/2 tsp. baking powder
1 cup sliced almonds	

Cream butter and sugar. Add almond extract, blend in egg. Mix flour and baking powder. Add to butter mixture. Stir dough with fork until smooth. Spread dough in greased 8 in. pan. Top with sliced almonds. Bake at 350°F/180°C for 30 minutes.

prize chocolate cake

1/4 cup butter
1/4 cup shortening
2 cups sugar
1 tsp. vanilla
2 eggs
3/4 tsp. baking soda
3/4 cup cocoa
1³/⁴ cup flour
3/4 tsp. baking powder
1/8 tsp. salt
1³/⁴ cups milk

Generously grease and flour two 9 in. round cake pans. Cream butter, shortening, sugar, and vanilla until light and fluffy. Blend in eggs. Combine baking soda, cocoa, flour, baking powder, and salt in bowl; add alternately with milk to batter. Blend well. Pour into prepared pans. Bake at 350°F/180°C for 30–35 minutes. Cool 10 minutes. Remove from pans.

no-bake chocolate peanut butter oatmeal cookies

2 cups sugar
1/2 cup milk
1/2 cup peanut butter
3¹/² cups oatmeal
1/4 cup cocoa
1 cup margarine
1 tsp. vanilla

Mix sugar, cocoa, milk, and margarine in heavy saucepan; bring to boil on high heat, stirring constantly. Reduce heat to medium boil for four minutes, stirring constantly. Remove from heat. Stir in peanut butter. Add vanilla and oats. Put in buttered 9 x 13 in. pan, or drop by spoonfuls onto wax paper. Let cool.

carrot cake

1$^{1/2}$ cups oil

2 cups sugar

1 cup chopped nuts

1 tsp. cinnamon

3 cups grated carrots

4 eggs

2 tsp. baking soda

2 cups flour

1 tsp. salt

Beat eggs, add oil and sugar. Mix dry ingredients with nuts. Add to egg mixture and stir in carrots. Bake in a 9 x 13 in. greased pan for 40 minutes at 350°F/180°C.

Frosting:

1/2 cup butter

2 cups powdered sugar

8 oz. cream cheese

1 tsp. vanilla

Blend butter and cream cheese, add powdered sugar and vanilla. Spread on cake.

peanut butter cookies

1 cup margarine

1 cup brown sugar

2 eggs

3 cups flour

1 tsp. vanilla

1 cup white sugar

1 cup peanut butter

2 tsp. baking powder

Cream margarine and add vanilla. Add sugars gradually, creaming well. Sift together flour and baking powder. Add beaten eggs to sugar and butter mixture. Add peanut butter, mix well. Add flour mixture slowly, mixing well. Roll into small balls. Place on greased cookie sheet. Flatten in crisscross pattern with fork dipped in water. Bake at 375°F/190°C for 10–15 minutes.

mcclung chocolate chip cookies

1 cup oil

1 cup brown sugar

2 eggs

2 cups flour

1 tsp. baking soda

1 cup nuts

1/2 cup margarine

1 cup white sugar

2 cups oatmeal

1/2 tsp. salt

18 oz. package chocolate chips

Combine oil, margarine, sugars, and eggs. Mix well. Add oatmeal, flour, salt, and soda; mix well. Stir in chocolate chips and nuts. Drop by teaspoonfuls on ungreased cookie sheet. Bake at 325°F/160°C for 12–15 minutes, or until light brown.

african cookies

150 grams (3/4 cup) brown sugar

150 grams (3/4 cup) dates, chopped

100 grams (1 cup) nuts, chopped

2 eggs, beaten

3 ml (1 tsp.) vanilla

500 ml. (2 cups) crispy rice cereal

In a large saucepan, mix sugar, eggs, and dates. Stir over medium heat for 5 minutes, or until mixture pulls away from edges of pan. Cook for another 3 minutes. Remove from heat and add vanilla and nuts. Fold in cereal. With buttered fingers, roll mixture into balls and set on wax paper. Allow to cool.

fruit pizza

1/2 cup butter

3/4 cup white sugar

2 Tb. milk

1/2 tsp. vanilla

$1^{3/4}$ cup flour

2 tsp. baking powder

1/2 tsp. salt

Mix ingredients together. Flatten dough onto 12-inch pizza pan and bake 10–15 minutes at 350°F/180°C. Cool.

Beat together:

8 oz. cream cheese   1/3 cup sugar

1/2 tsp. almond flavoring

Spread over crust and arrange fruit on top.

Top with glaze:

1/2 cup fruit juice   1 tsp. cornstarch

1 Tb. water

Mix together in saucepan and cook over medium heat to boil. Remove from heat and cool slightly. Spoon over fruit (to keep fruit from turning brown).

pavlova

$1^{1/2}$ cups sugar   4 Tb. boiling water

1 tsp. vanilla   2 large egg whites

1 tsp. white vinegar

Beat ingredients together until stiff peaks form. Pile onto a wet baking sheet and cook for $1^{1/2}$ hours at 200°F/100°C. Top with whipped cream and fruit.

mango pie

1 cup sugar   3/4 cup whipping cream

3 Tb. flour   1/4 tsp. cinnamon

5 fresh mangoes, cut up

Preheat oven to 450°F/230°C. Prepare pastry from favorite recipe.

Stir together sugar and flour; spread half of mixture in pastry shell. Place mangos cut side down on sugar mixture, and sprinkle rest of sugar mixture over fruit. Pour cream on mangoes; sprinkle cinnamon on top. Cover with foil and bake 10 minutes. Reduce heat to 350°F/180°C. Bake 30–35 minutes longer. Remove foil for last 5 minutes of baking.

mashed potatoes

9 large potatoes
1 cup sour cream
1 tsp. salt
1/4 tsp. pepper

8 oz. cream cheese
2 tsp. onion salt
2 Tb. butter

Peel and cook potatoes. Mash until smooth. Add remaining ingredients and beat until fluffy. Place in 9 x 13 in. buttered pan. Bake at 350°F/180°C for 30 minutes.

fondue gruyère

1 clove garlic
2 Tb. kirsch per person
1 Tb. cornstarch

1/2 lb. Gruyère cheese per person
1/2 cup dry white wine per person
pepper to taste

Rub inside of fondue pot with garlic. Place shredded cheese in pot. Pour wine over cheese. Place pot over high heat and heat cheese, stirring slowly but constantly with wooden spoon. Dissolve the cornstarch into the kirsch. When cheese mixture starts to boil, add cornstarch mixture. Add pepper. Remove from high heat to table unit, making sure fondue keeps bubbling lightly.

Other cheese options: for four servings, use 1 lb. Swiss (Emmental) cheese or 1/2 lb. Swiss with 1/2 lb. Gruyère.

polynesian baked chicken

2 frying chickens, cut up
1 cup flour

1/2 tsp. salt

for the sauce:
1 tsp. salt
1/2 lb. melted butter
1 cup orange juice
2 Tb. lemon juice
1 Tb. cornstarch

1/2 cup brown sugar
1 Tb. soy sauce
2 cups fresh papaya
1 Tb. sesame seeds

Shake chicken in bag with flour and 1 tsp. salt. Coat inside of baking dish with 2 Tb. of the melted butter. Put chicken in dish and brush with remaining melted butter. Bake 50 minutes at 350°F/180°C or until chicken is browned. To prepare sauce, combine juices, sugar, soy sauce, 1/2 tsp. salt, and cornstarch in saucepan. Bring to boil, stirring constantly. When sauce is clear and thickened, remove from heat and add papaya and sesame seeds. Pour sauce over chicken and bake 10 minutes longer.

habona's swahili chicken

1 chicken, cut up	2 large onions, chopped or sliced
2 sticks cinnamon	6–10 cloves garlic
1/2 cup plain yogurt	2 Tb. margarine
6 oz. (small can) tomato paste	1 in. ginger root, peeled and crushed
1 small bunch parsley	

Melt margarine, add onions, and fry until medium brown. Crush spices, using a liquefier or food processor. Stir spices into onions and cook for 2–3 minutes. Add tomato paste and yogurt. Cook slowly for 1 hour. Meanwhile, fry chicken until golden brown and tender. Add chicken to onion mixture and cook until heated thoroughly.

beef curry

1$^{1/2}$ Tb. oil	1 onion, sliced in rings
2–3 tsp. curry powder	1$^{1/2}$ lbs. lean flank steak, cut in 1 in. cubes
4 oz. can mushrooms	1 tomato, diced
1 clove garlic	1 tsp. salt
2 tsp. sugar	cooked rice

Heat oil in heavy skillet. Sauté onion. Stir in curry powder and cook 1 minute. Add steak cubes and cook until slightly browned. Add enough boiling water to barely cover cubes, about 2 cups. Cover and simmer about 2 hours or until beef is extremely tender. Thicken with mixture of 2 Tb. cornstarch and 2 Tb. water. Serve beef on a bed of rice, and set out curry accompaniments: tomato wedges, raisins, chopped peanuts, sautéed onions, pineapple chunks, flaked coconut, papaya, oranges, sweet pickles, and/or bananas.

curry rice with apples, raisins, and almonds

1 red or green apple, chopped
1/4 cup light raisins
1 small onion, chopped
1/4 tsp. salt
1¼ cups water
parsley sprigs for garnish

1/4 cup dark raisins
1/4 cup sliced almonds
1/2 Tb. curry powder
1 cup white rice
2 tsp. oil

Combine fruits and nuts in a small bowl. Over medium heat, sauté onion and curry powder until soft. Stir in rice and salt, and cook for a few minutes more. Transfer mixture to a medium size saucepan. Add water. Sprinkle apple, raisin, and almond mixture over top of the rice. Bring to a boil, cover, and simmer on low heat for 20–25 minutes. Remove lid and scoop out with a 1/2-cup measure, turning onto plates in mounds. Garnish each mound with a sprig of parsley tucked into the rice. Serves 6.

lasagna

1 pound ground beef
1 clove garlic
2 Tb. parsley flakes
3 cups cottage cheese
2 eggs, beaten
1 Tb. dried parsley
1/2 tsp. pepper

2 cups tomatoes
1½ tsp. salt
1 Tb. basil
12 oz. uncooked lasagna noodles
1/2 cup Parmesan cheese
2 tsp. salt
1/2 pound mozzarella cheese

Brown meat slowly; drain grease. Add tomatoes, garlic, 1½ tsp. salt, 2 Tb. parsley flakes, and basil. Simmer uncovered 30 minutes. Cook noodles, drain, and rinse. Combine cottage cheese with eggs, Parmesan cheese, 1 Tb. parsley, 2 tsp. salt, and pepper. Place half of the noodles in greased 9 x 13 in. pan. Spread with half the cottage cheese mixture, half the mozzarella cheese, and half the meat sauce. Repeat. Bake at 375°F/190°C for 30 minutes. Garnish with mozzarella cheese. Let stand 10 minutes before serving. Serves 12.

chili

1 pound ground beef	one 8 oz. can tomato soup
1 oz. can whole tomatoes	1 large onion
1 Tb. chili powder	1 Tb. paprika
1/4 tsp. Worcestershire sauce	1 15 oz. can kidney beans
dash of Tabasco	salt and pepper to taste

Brown meat; drain. Mix with remaining ingredients and simmer on stove for 2 hours. Serves 10.

SALADS

sweet-sour cucumbers

1/2 cup white vinegar	1/3 cup salad oil
2 Tb. sugar	1 tsp. salt
1/4 tsp. white pepper	1/4 tsp. dried oregano leaves
3 medium cucumbers, thinly sliced	

One hour before serving or up to two days ahead: In large bowl, combine all ingredients. Cover and refrigerate at least 45 minutes to blend flavors, stirring mixture occasionally. Serve with hamburgers, frankfurters, fried or broiled fish, or chicken. Makes 12 servings.

avocado and tomato salad

6 slices bacon	3 Tb. oil
1 Tb. vinegar	1/2 tsp. salt
1/8 tsp. pepper	3 drops red pepper sauce
2 medium avocados, cubed	2 medium tomatoes, cubed
1 small onion, chopped	

Mix all ingredients and refrigerate 2 hours before serving. Serves 6–8.

hawaiian chicken salad

3 cups cooked chicken, chopped
1 cup cubed celery
1 tart apple, peeled and chopped
1 can (11 oz.) mandarin oranges
1/2 cup macadamia nuts
1 cup mayonnaise
2 tsp. curry powder
1 tsp. salt

Combine all ingredients and chill for at least two hours. Serves 8–10.

potato salad

6 medium boiled potatoes
1 cup finely diced celery
1/4 cup minced parsley
1/2 tsp. salt
1 tsp. vinegar
2 tsp. mustard
1 tsp. minced onion
3 hard-cooked eggs, chopped
1/4 cup shredded carrots
1/8 tsp. pepper
1/2–3/4 cup mayonnaise

Combine potatoes, onion, celery, eggs, parsley, and carrots. Separately, combine salt, pepper, vinegar, mayonnaise, and mustard. Add to the potato mixture and toss well. Serves 10–12.

broccoli salad

2 bunches broccoli, chopped
1/2 cup raisins
1/4 tsp. sugar
2 Tb. white vinegar
1/2 pound bacon, fried and crumbled
1/2 cup onions, chopped
1 cup mayonnaise

Mix ingredients together and refrigerate for at least 1 hour. Serves 8–10.

taco salad

1 onion, chopped	4 tomatoes, chopped
1 head of lettuce, chopped	1/4 pound cheddar cheese, grated
8 oz. French dressing	1 medium-size bag tortilla chips
1 large avocado, sliced	1 pound hamburger
1 15 oz. can kidney beans, drained	

Combine chopped onion, tomato, and head of lettuce in bowl. Add cheddar cheese and French dressing and toss. Add tortilla chips and avocado. Brown hamburger and drain grease. Add kidney beans and simmer meat and beans about 10 minutes. Add meat mixture to salad while still warm. Serves 10.

melon fruit salad

3 different types of melons	1/4 cup oil
2 Tb. honey	1 Tb. lemon juice

Cut melon into balls or cubes. Mix oil, honey, and lemon juice. Toss with melon.

fruit kebabs

Use seasonal fresh fruit. Dice any variety of fruit and put on wooden skewers.

MISCELLANEOUS RECIPES

piña colada punch

2 cans pineapple juice	1 can coconut syrup
1 can evaporated milk	

Blend together in a blender until smooth. Serve with ice.

apple dip

1/2 cup brown sugar
1 tsp. cinnamon
dash nutmeg

8 oz. cream cheese
1 tsp. vanilla
apples

Beat brown sugar, cream cheese, cinnamon, vanilla, and nutmeg together. Serve as a dip for apples slices.

corn syrup

1 cup sugar
1 Tb. corn flour or cornstarch

1 cup water

Mix in saucepan and boil 5 minutes at rolling boil. Cool before using. Use in recipes calling for corn syrup or Karo syrup.

sweetened condensed milk

2/3 cup sugar
1/3 cup boiling water

1 cup powdered milk
3 tsp. butter, melted

Combine all ingredients and beat until smooth. Store in refrigerator until ready to use.

mock sour cream

1 cup cottage cheese
dash of salt

1 Tb. lemon juice
1 Tb. skim milk

In food processor or blender, whirl all ingredients at high speed until smooth. Makes one cup.

mayonnaise

2 tsp. sugar

1 egg

1 tsp. salt

2 tsp. white vinegar

1 tsp. mustard

2 cups vegetable oil

Beat together sugar, vinegar, egg, mustard, and salt. Add oil very slowly, almost dripping it in.

play dough

1 cup flour

1 cup water

2 tsp. cream of tartar

1/2 cup salt

1 Tb. oil

food coloring

Mix in a saucepan and cook over medium heat until hot and clear right through. Cool and knead, adding more flour if necessary.

recipe for gracious hospitality

Measure 1 cup of friendly words, carefully chosen

Add 2 heaping cups of understanding

4 full tablespoons of time

5 full tablespoons of patience

1/2 cup of warmth

Stir in a dash of humor. Mix well and simmer slowly all day long.
Serve ample helpings of happiness to your guests.

acknowledgments

My thanks to my parents, Fred and Glenda Polinder, for modeling hospitality my whole life through. To Loren and Darlene Cunningham, who believed in me and allowed me to express hospitality on their behalf to those who entered their home and lives for many years. To my YWAM women heroes: Carol Boyd, Romkje Fountain, Sally McClung, Judy Orred, and Eva Spengler, who recognized a gift in me and encouraged me to express it. To Adele Noetzelman, who put into words my heart and passion for hospitality. And finally to my husband, Arnold, and my children—Nathan, Daniella, and Mia—for their patience, encouragement, and the desire to grow and live out the ministry of hospitality.

about the authors

DEBBIE ROTTIER joined YWAM in 1982, when God called her to minister in the area of hospitality to "serve the saints." Since then she has served in YWAM in Hawaii, the Netherlands, Indonesia, Uganda, Switzerland, Denmark, Montana, and South Africa. Debbie has managed ministry hospitality departments, run hospitality seminars, and provided oversight to hospitality teams for major events and conferences throughout YWAM. She has a special heart for missionary moms. Debbie, her husband, Arnold, and their three children serve together in YWAM.

ADELE NOETZELMAN is a freelance writer and editor who has served in YWAM and several other ministries in the United States and overseas. She and her husband, Jim, live in Washington State on a family farm they share with their adult children and grandchildren.